Practicing Recursion with JavaFX

Irena Pevac

DEDICATION

This book is dedicated to Slobodanka Jankovic

ACKNOWLEDGMENTS

The author is deeply grateful to John Lewis for reading the preliminary version of this text and providing numerous useful comments and words of encouragement. Thanks also to student Paulo Nunes for his diligent work to improve the presentation of problems.

PREFACE

Educators and students consider recursion one of the most difficult topics in introductory programming courses. The limited number of recursive examples in the textbooks is not sufficient for most students. The author has been providing additional examples of recursive code to learners, and after more practicing majority improved their knowledge of the topic significantly. That was the inspiration to write this book.

The text is aimed primarily at students in CS I or CS II courses, who can use it to practice outside of class time at their own pace. It may be helpful for instructors teaching those courses, as well. For them it can serve as a poll of test examples, or as a base to create projects that include variations of existing methods.

The book provides collection of over 150 examples. Ninety percent of the problems are potential questions on the tests or final exams. The remaining ten percent of the problems are for advanced students who grasped the topic and like to be challenged to do more. Each example includes a problem specified in English, solution at the algorithm level, and recursive code implemented in Java. Graphics examples have picture of the outcome that should be drawn in addition to code. The book is divided into six chapters and covers recursive examples on integers, arrays, linked lists, linked trees, and graphical examples. It is revised edition of the book *Practicing Recursion in Java* CreateSpace 2016. Chapter 6 is completely redone due to significant changes in Java language related to graphics. Graphics examples are done in JavaFX.

Writing code recursively requires a paradigm shift. Learners are used to implement iteration with loops, where steps are specified in the order how they are performed, and now have to learn to specify solution for such problems implicitly. We start with recursive examples on integers, arrays, and linked lists despite the fact that those examples can be done iteratively in more efficient way. Using simple examples is favorable because obtaining solutions recursively for those examples is much easier than obtaining solutions recursively for more complex examples such as those involving trees or graphs. Learners start by writing recursive code for simple examples where the main challenge is to grasp the new way of formulating the solution for the given problem by using solution for one or more subproblems and specifying the base case where solution can be specified explicitly. This approach later facilitates a smooth transition to writing code recursively on more advanced data structures.

Chapter 1   Introduction

The first chapter provides overview of recursive way of thinking and illustrates base case and recursive steps on several algorithms. Some important and more difficult to follow algorithms such as Tower of Hanoi and determining the n-th Fibonacci number are provided with the trace of their execution. Finally, some typical mistakes that learners make while practicing are outlined.

Chapter 2 Recursive examples on integers

The second chapter contains problems that use an integer parameter. Some examples are to calculate the sum of first n integer numbers, calculate the sum of first n cubes, calculate the sum of first n reciprocal numbers, determine the number of digits in the given integer, print given sentence or phrase n times, compute all permutations for given positive integer, compute all subsets of the set {1, 2,…, n} and similar.

Chapter 3 Recursive examples on arrays

The third chapter contains problems that use an array parameter and integer parameter n which represents array's actual size. Actual size n is the number of occupied positions in the array, while array's size is maximum number of components that array can store. Some examples covered here are: determine the sum of all components for an array of integer type, determine whether array is sorted in ascending order, count the number of components in the array that have value equal to given item that matches the array's data type, determine the largest item in the array, sort array by using insertion, selection, bubble sort, binary and ternary search for given key and similar.

Chapter 4 Recursive examples on linked lists

The fourth chapter contains problems on linked lists. Some examples cover problems that are included in the section on arrays. However, in this chapter those problems are implemented assuming that linked list of items is given. We provide three different implementation approaches. Some of the problems included are: determine reference to the node with smallest data, determine if corresponding data in a given linked lists and another linked list that is passed as a parameter are the same, insert an item into sorted linked list and similar.

Chapter 5 Recursive examples on trees

The fifth chapter contains problems that work on linked trees. Some of the examples covered in this chapter are: count the number of leaves in a given tree, count the number of positive non-leaves in a given tree, return the reference to a node with the largest data item, return the depth of a tree, determine if given item is in the tree, determine if given tree is binary search tree, and similar.

Chapter 6 Recursive graphical examples

The sixth chapter contains problems to draw given picture. Each example is specified in English, followed by resulting picture, and complete application implemented in JavaFX. Examples included in this chapter draw parallel and vertical lines, concentric circles, concentric squares filled with alternating colors, spiral, snail, stairs, Sierpinski triangles, C-curve, Dragon-curve, Broccoli-curve, Butterfly-squares and similar.

Irena Pevac

CONTENTS

CHAPTER 1   INTRODUCTION

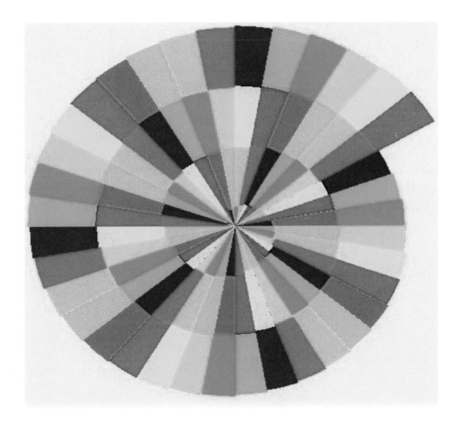

Overview of implementing recursive algorithms

Examples of base cases and recursive steps, algorithm tracing, and typical mistakes

Recursion is a powerful programming tool. Problems suitable for recursion are solved by referring back to the same steps used in solving the original problem. An alternative to iteration, recursion requires knowledge of how an original task can be completed using one or more subtasks of the same type. It allows programmers to write elegant and shorter code to perform various tasks on advanced data structures such as trees and graphs.

Recursive solutions are expressed in terms of one subproblem or some combination of several subproblems of the same type as the original problem, or the solution to the problem is straightforward and can be easily stated explicitly without referring to a subproblem. A subproblem is a similar but simpler version of the original problem. For example, when the original problem P depends upon some integer parameter n, denoted P(n), the subproblem might be P(n - 1), or P(n - 2), or P(n / 2), or some combination of the above. The subproblem is the same as the original task, but usually has an argument that is smaller than n.

Recursive methods can be direct or indirect. Direct recursive methods are those that invoke the same method in the code definition. Indirect recursive method A might invoke method B in its code, while method B invokes method A again. In this book we will limit our examples to direct recursion.

Let us compare the task to print the numbers from 1 to n performed iteratively and recursively.

1.1 Iterative approach vs. Recursive approach

In the iterative approach, one starts by printing the number 1, then the number 2, and at the end print the number n. The n steps, each one printing one of the numbers, are performed using some sort of loop.

```
// PRECONDITION: n positive
public void printNumbers (int n)
{
    for (int counter = 1; counter <= n; counter++)
      System.out.println(counter);
}
```

Using the recursive approach, we say that for positive *n*, performing the task of printing the numbers from 1 to *n*, will be achieved by performing first a subtask to print the numbers from 1 to *n*-1, and then printing the number *n*. Printing the numbers from 1 to *n*-1 is the same problem as the original one, so we may invoke the same method with the argument *n*-1.

```
// PRECONDITION: n positive
public void print1toN(int n)
{
    if (n == 1)
      System.out.println(1);
    else
    {
       print1toN(n-1);
       System.out.println(n);
    }
}
```

In the method `print1toN`, when *n* equals 1, the number 1 is printed and that completes the job. That is called a base case or a stopping case. The precondition specifies the facts that must be fulfilled when the method is invoked. Since *n* must be positive, if it is not one it must be greater than one. For *n* that is greater than one, two lines of code are performed. The first line is the invocation of the same method recursively to print the numbers from 1 to *n*-1. The second line prints the last number *n*. When both steps are executed the job is completed. The first line, however, is not a single step. In order to execute the first line, several subsequent invocations, each one with an argument 1 less than the argument at the invocation of the previous level, will be performed until the base case is reached. That is called the recursive step.

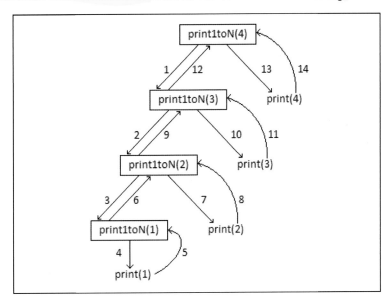

Figure 1   Trace for print1toN(4)

Rectangles show method invocations and labels on arcs specify the order of performing steps in time. When the actual parameter n equals 4, the code requires the execution of print1toN(3), and after that prints n which equals 4. The execution of print1toN(3) with the actual parameter n being 3 requires the execution of print1toN (2), and after that prints number n which is 3. The execution of print1toN(2) with the actual parameter n being 2 requires the execution of print1toN (1), and after that prints the number n which is 2. The execution of print1toN(1) with the actual parameter $n=1$ prints the number n which is 1. After completing print1toN(1) at level $n=2$, the number 2 is printed. This completes the execution of print1toN(2) at level $n=3$, and the number 3 is printed. This completes the execution of print1toN(3) at level $n=4$, and the last number 4 is printed. This completes the execution of print1toN(4).

In summary, the two important parts of recursive methods are:

- Base case
- Recursive step

Base case refers to the part of the code that provides an answer to the problem or specifies explicitly what should be done without referring to any subproblem. It specifies what the answer is, or tells what steps, if any, should be performed. Sometimes the base case (also called stopping case) might be hidden if nothing needs to be done in the base case.

When the recursive method has an integer parameter, the base case is usually the smallest integer value for which the problem makes sense. Most often that is either 0 or 1. Base case is also called stopping case, because it provides code which has to be executed and completes the execution of the method. No further calls or actions are needed. The base case is always the part of the code where the solution to the problem is easy to state, as opposed to the recursive step where we refer to one or more recursive subproblems and combine them somehow in order to complete the original task.

1.2 Examples of base cases and recursive steps for several problems

1.2.1   Factorial

The factorial, $n!$, for a given number n is mathematically defined for numbers that are either equal to zero or are positive integers. Mathematicians define factorial as follows:

$$n! = \begin{cases} 1 & \text{if } n = 0 \\ n\,(n-1)! & \text{if } n > 0 \end{cases}$$

In the simplest case, when n equals 0, it is possible to give a straightforward answer. The result to be returned is 1. So, the base case is when n equals 0, and the code performed for the base case is **return 1;** The value 0 is the smallest integer for which a factorial is mathematically defined. A recursive step is performed when $n > 0$. It includes an invocation of **factorial(n-1)** and the result of it should be multiplied by n in order to determine **factorial(n)**.

Not every true mathematical equation involving a factorial is suitable for a recursive step. For instance, the equation $n! = (n+1)! / (n+1)$ is mathematically correct, but using it to implement the recursive step would not allow completion since each time it would take us further away from the base case, so the process would not terminate.

The recursive step always follows the domain dependent relationship between the problem and one or more subproblem(s). The subproblem(s) should always direct the process toward one of the base cases to ensure termination.

1.2.2 Sum of the first n numbers

The next example is to determine, recursively, the sum of the first n numbers for a given number n. This problem assumes that n is a positive integer. The base case is when n equals 1. The entire sum also equals 1. So, the code in the base case is to return 1. The recursive step is performed when $n > 1$. It includes the invocation of Sum(n-1) to get sum $1 + 2 + ... + (n-1)$, and the result of it should be increased by n. The above follows from the equation

$$1 \ + \ 2 \ + \ ... \ + \ (n-1) \ + \ n \ = \ (1 \ + \ 2 \ + \ ... \ + \ (n-1)) \ + \ n$$

1.2.3 Traverse linked list

In this example, the task is to traverse a linked list referred to by a reference, *list*. The base case is when the reference, *list*, equals null. This means that the list is empty. In that case, there is nothing to traverse and our task is already completed. That means that there is no code when the list is empty. This is the so called hidden base case.

Instead of writing	We write it in the following way:

`if (list == null)`
  //*no code to be executed*
`else`
  //*code to be performed to traverse nonempty list*
	`if (list != null)`
	  // *code to be performed to traverse nonempty list*

The else clause is omitted since there is nothing to be done in such a case anyway. The recursive step includes code to visit and display data stored in the first node, and a recursive invocation of the traversal method for the sublist that starts at the successor after the first node.

// Display the data in the first node.
// Traverse the sublist that starts at the successor node.

We provide different ways to implement this example in Chapter 4.

The next examples illustrate recursive examples with more than one base case, and/or more than one recursive calls. Several recursive calls in the body of the method lead to duplicate computations since the computer does not have the ability to memorize previously computed values for instant retrieval when called upon, but rather, those values must be recomputed as needed. Observe the recursion tree generated by the hand-trace, noticing the duplicate computations that must be made.

1.2.4 Tower of Hanoi example

The Tower of Hanoi is a classic example where recursion allows us to express the problem easily. Legend has it that monks in a temple of Brahma were given three golden rods. The first rod has a stack of 64 disks. The largest disk is at the bottom, and the smallest is on the top. Each disk on the stack is smaller than the one on which it is sitting. The other two rods are empty at the beginning. The goal is to reposition all 64 disks from the first rod onto the third rod by moving only one disk at a time. At no time should a larger disk be placed on top of a smaller one. Legend has it that the world would end upon completion of the above task. Assuming that moving a disk from one rod to another takes one second, and that monks work without resting nor ever making a mistake, their work would take more than 500,000 million years, which is 25 times the estimated age of our universe.

The starting position has 64 (or n in general) disks on the first rod, and the other two rods are empty. The final position has 64 (or n in general) disks on the third rod, and the other two are empty. The task will be completed if we perform the following:

- Move 63 (or n-1 in general) disks from the first rod to the second rod;
- Move one disk from the first rod to the third rod;
- Move 63 (or n-1 in general) disks from the second rod to the third rod.

The first and the third part are both subproblems with one disk less than the original problem. Thus, the entire method can be coded easily as follows. The three rods will be named `from`, `aux`, and `dest` to indicate their role in the original problem. We will not provide code to actually move the disks. The printout that the top disk from rod x should be moved to rod y will be provided instead. If there is only one disk, then that should be moved from the `from` position to the `dest` position. If the number of disks is larger than one, we perform the above-mentioned three subtasks.

```
public void hanoi( int n, char from, char aux, char dest)
{
    if (n == 1)
        System.out.println( from + " -> " + dest);
    else
    {
        Hanoi(n-1, from, dest, aux);
        System.out.println( from + " -> " + dest);
        Hanoi(n-1, aux, from, dest);
    }
}
```

However, it is not trivial to trace the execution of moves. Let us trace the steps for the method call with 3 disks. hanoi(3, *a*, *b*, *c*) will be completed if we do the following: do the subtask hanoi(2, *a*, *c*, *b*), move the largest disk from *a* to *c*, and do the subtask hanoi(2, *b*, *a*, *c*). Each of the recursive calls with 2 disks will require additional calls as specified above. In time, the moves are performed from top to bottom as listed.

Using the instructions of how to move the top disk from rod *x* to rod *y*, the task hanoi(3, *a*, *b*, *c*) will be completed as follows.

```
hanoi(3, a, b, c)
        hanoi(2, a, c, b)
                hanoi(1, a, b, c)              a -> c
                Print    a -> b                a -> b
                hanoi(1, c, a, b)             c -> b
        Print    a -> c                        a -> c
        hanoi(2, b, a, c)
                hanoi(1, b, c, a)             b -> a
                Print b -> c                  b -> c
                hanoi(1, a, b, c)             a -> c
```

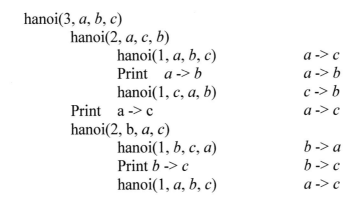

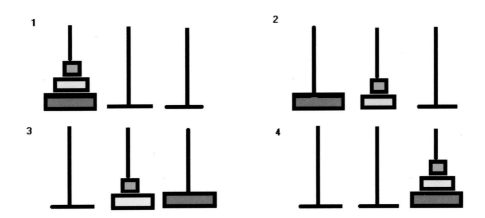

Figure 2 hanoi (3, *a*, *b*, *c*) subtasks

Step 1 in Figure 2 is the starting state for hanoi(3, *a*, *b*, *c*)
Step 2 is the state achieved after completing subtask hanoi(2, *a*, *c*, *b*).
Step 3 is the state achieved after completing subtask   print *a* -> *c*.
Step 4 is the goal state that is achieved after completing hanoi(2, *b*, *a*, *c*).

Figure 3 shows a graphical illustration of the actual steps performed in hanoi(3, *a*, *b*, *c*). The code only provides the following printout:

$a \rightarrow c$
$a \rightarrow b$
$c \rightarrow b$
$a \rightarrow c$
$b \rightarrow a$
$b \rightarrow c$
$a \rightarrow c$

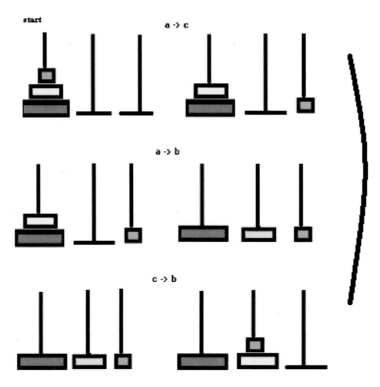

Subproblem of moving the top two disks from rod a to rod b

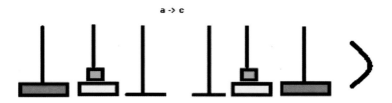

Moving one (the largest) disk from a to c

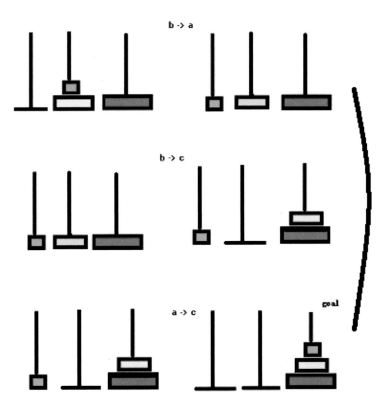

Subproblem of moving the top two disks from rod b to rod c

Figure 3   Actual steps performed in Tower of Hanoi given 3 disks

1.2.5   Fibonacci sequence

The Fibonacci sequence of numbers was introduced by the Italian mathematician Fibonacci in the twelfth century. Here is the story that gives the background for the Fibonacci numbers.

- Suppose that we start with a pair of rabbits, one male and one female.
- Rabbits mature for breeding in two months.
- Also assume that no rabbits ever die, and every pair of rabbits produces a pair of offspring (male + female) each month after maturity.

The n-th Fibonacci number corresponds to the number of pairs at the n-th month. For the first two months there is only one pair of rabbits. In month 3, the first pair matures and produces another pair, so there are two pairs. In month 4, the first pair produces another pair of offspring, so there are 3 pairs of rabbits. In month five the first offspring pair is also mature so, there are two additional pairs of offspring, i.e. 5 pairs. The number of pairs at each month will generate the Fibonacci sequence.

It is easy to see that the first and second Fibonacci numbers are equal to 1, and each consecutive number is the sum of the previous two numbers. The first six Fibonacci numbers are 1, 1, 2, 3, 5, and 8, and the seventh Fibonacci number, fib(7), is the sum of fib(6), the sixth number, and fib(5), the fifth number in the sequence.

Now we can formally identify the base case and the recursive step. There are two base cases, fib(1) = 1 and fib(2) = 1. For numbers $n > 2$, fib(n) = fib(n - 1) + fib(n - 2). Let's look at the java implementation of this recursive method.

```
public int fib(int n)
{
    if (n <= 2)                       // base case
        return 1;
    else                              // recursive step
        return fib(n-1) + fib(n-2);
}
```

Note that within the method definition there are two separate invocations, fib(n-1) and fib(n-2). That makes it less efficient. The following tree traces the computation of fib(5) and illustrates this problem. For example, fib(3) with the entire subtree of calls is performed twice. Clearly this greatly increases execution time.

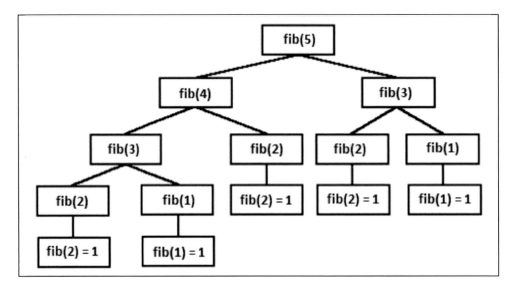

Figure 4 Trace of fib(5) invocations

There is significantly more duplication of effort for a larger n. It would be ideal if the recursion process could remember the result of computing the intermediate steps, however, it does not! So, it recomputes the same invocation more than once. Trace the execution for fib(10). How many times is fib(5) invoked?

1.2.6   Test if a list is sorted in ascending order

This example has three base cases. The first two are when the list is empty and when the list has only one element (singleton list). In both such cases the boolean value true is returned. The third base case is when the list has more than one element and the last component is smaller than its predecessor. In such a case the boolean value false is returned. The recursive step returns the same truth value as the recursive subproblem that tests if the sublist of the first n-1 list components is sorted in ascending order. In Chapter 3 we provide code for this example for a list given as an array and in Chapter 4 we do it for linked list.

1.3 Why recursion if iteration is more efficient

In most cases discussed so far, except the Tower of Hanoi example, the recursive approach can be replaced with iteration using a loop instead. It is even more efficient to use iteration. Recursion requires several calls before reaching the base case. Each invocation requires putting the method name and parameters on the activation stack, and upon completion, removing it from the stack when the results are passed back. This requires extra space and time. Recursion becomes even more inefficient when a method has two or more recursive invocations.

Why are we starting to practice recursion by writing code for examples on integers, arrays, and linked lists when those examples can be done iteratively in a more efficient way? Writing code recursively requires a paradigm shift from being used to specifying the steps explicitly, in the order how they are performed, to specifying them implicitly. The general pattern of recursive methods is as follows:

```
In one or more special cases the given problem is solved by
    Doing the base case(s) step without referring to any subproblem
else{
    Problem will be solved if one or more solution(s) for the subproblem(s) are combined
    somehow with optional additional steps needed to complete the original task.
}
```

We start with simple examples because obtaining solutions recursively for those examples is easier than obtaining solutions recursively for more complex examples such as those involving trees or graphs where recursion leads naturally to simple and elegant code. Learners should start by learning to write recursive code for simple examples where the main challenge is to grasp the new way of formulating the solution for the given problem recursively. This facilitates a smooth transition to writing code recursively on more advanced data structures.

1.4 Avoiding typical mistakes

Next we list some of the typical mistakes that learners make.

- Many learners who were exposed to iterative programming with loops before learning recursion tend to apply loops in addition to making calls to recursive subproblem(s). Problems where iterative code has a single loop do not require any loop when implemented with recursion. Problems such as selection sort, where iterative code has a nested loop, may keep one loop and use recursion to replace the other loop.

- Sometimes recursive algorithms have more than one base case, and learners forget one or more of them.

- Just like in the iterative approach, there is a difference between the methods that return a primitive type or some object and methods that return void. Methods that return void are invoked as a line of code. Methods that return either a primitive type or an object should never be invoked as a line of code since, in such cases, whatever they return is lost. Methods that return a primitive type should be invoked at the same places in the code where a variable of that primitive data type can be used. Methods that return some kind of object should be invoked at the same places in the code where a variable of that data type can be used. Learners often forget that and invoke a recursive subproblem as a line of code. Despite the fact that a recursive subproblem invocation is executed, whatever that subproblem returned is lost because it was not used and not assigned to a variable.

- Another typical mistake happens when learners do not cover all possibilities, and provide code for some cases but do not specify what should be done otherwise. For example, if the problem is to count students with a GPA above 3.0 in an array with n students, learners often return 0 if the list is empty, return 1 plus the result of the recursive call to the subproblem where the subarray contains the first n-1 students if the last component in the array is a student with a GPA above 3.0, and forget to specify what should be returned in the case when the last student does not have a GPA above 3.0.

- Finally, various logical mistakes can be made when the results of one or more recursive calls to subproblems are not combined properly to produce the correct answer to original problem.

CHAPTER 2   EXAMPLES ON INTEGERS

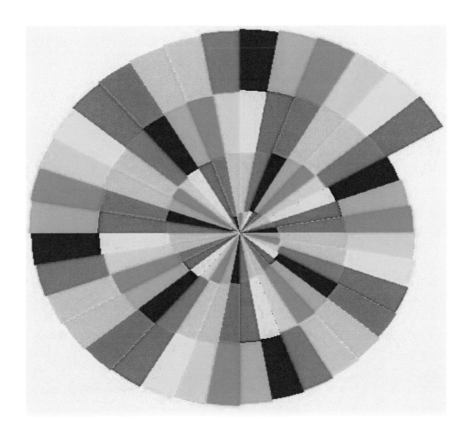

Recursive methods with an integer input parameter

Examples include sum of first n numbers, convert number from base 10 to base 2, return all permutations of n numbers, print triangular shapes, and similar.

In the next several chapters we provide practice examples of coding recursive methods dealing with integers, arrays, linked lists, binary trees, and graphics.

This chapter is devoted to examples with integers. Often we provide several algorithms for the same problem. Solutions for respective problems at algorithm level are given first, followed by an implementation in Java. We highly recommend that learners try to write the code for the method independently. In case of problems, the algorithm should be checked first, and then try again. At the end learner should compare its own solution with the Java implementation provided in the book.

Most methods have preconditions. Those are facts that must be true when method is invoked. The code provides correct outcome only when all specified preconditions are meet.

When one writes a method to do some task recursively, one must discern two things. First, one must determine an initial value or several values, called the base case, for which we can specify the result or answer for the task explicitly without calling the any subproblem. Usually the base case is when n has either value 0, 1, or 2, or the base case has several initial values. Second, one must determine the recursive step that specifies how this original problem can be solved or performed by using one or more subproblems. When the original problem has parameter n, the subproblem has value n decreased either by a constant or by a constant factor (usually $n - 1$, $n - 2$, or $n / 2$, $n / 10$, or similar).

The subproblem should be a simpler version of the original problem, which is closer to the base case. Some recursive examples may define the solution by combining two or more subproblems.

EXAMPLES

1) Given a positive integer value n, write a method to print "Hello" n times.

ALGORITHM 1:

When *n* is one, print "Hello". Otherwise, print "Hello" and then call the same method recursively to print "Hello" *n*-1 times.

```java
// PRECONDITION: n positive integer
void printHello(int n)
{
    if (n == 1)
      System.out.println("Hello");
    else
    {
        System.out.println("Hello");
        printHello(n - 1);
    }
}
```

ALGORITHM 2 :

When *n* is positive, print "Hello", and next, call the method recursively to print "Hello" *n*-1 times. This has shorter code but it makes one more recursive call than the first one.

```java
// PRECONDITION: n positive integer
void printHello(int n)
{
    if (n > 0)
    {
        System.out.println("Hello");
        printHello(n - 1);
    }
}
```

 2) For a given positive integer number *n* write a method to print numbers from 1 to *n*. For instance, for *n* equal to 5 the outcome is 1 2 3 4 5.

ALGORITHM:

If *n* equals 1, that value should be displayed; otherwise, the recursive call with parameter *n*-1 should display numbers from 1 to *n*-1, and then *n* should be displayed.

```
// PRECONDITION:  n positive
void print_1TOn(int n)
{
    if (n == 1)
      System.out.println("1");
    else
    {
       print_1TOn(n-1);
       System.out.print(n);
    }
}
```

3) For a given positive integer number *n* write a method to print numbers from *n* down to 1. For instance, for *n* equal to 5 the outcome is 5 4 3 2 1.

ALGORITHM:

If *n* equals 1, that value should be displayed; otherwise, *n* should be displayed and then the recursive call with parameter *n*-1 should display numbers from n-1 down to 1.
NOTE: Just changing the order of steps to display current value of n and calling recursive subproblem in example 2, prints numbers in reverse order in example 3. The tree, such as shown in the introduction, to trace the execution, can be used to verify that.

```
// PRECONDITION:  n positive
void print_nDownto1(int n)
{
    if (n == 1)
      System.out.println("1");
    else
    {
       System.out.print(n);
       print_nDownto1(n-1);
    }
}
```

4 - 6) Write a method to compute the value of a positive real value *a* raised to a power *n*, such that *n* is nonnegative. Consider the cases specified by the following formulas.

ALGORITHM 1:

Raise a number *a* to a power *n*, by using the following definition:

$$a^n = 1, \qquad\qquad \text{if } n = 0,$$
$$a^n = a * a^{n-1} \qquad\qquad \text{if } n > 0.$$

When n equals 0, power is 1; otherwise, use the result for the subproblem, that has n reduced by one, and multiply it with a in order to obtain result.

```
// PRECONDITIONS: n nonnegative integer, a number of type double, a and n not both zero.
double power1(double a, int n)
{
   if (n == 0)
      return 1.0;
   else if (n > 0)
      return a * power1(a, n-1);
}
```

ALGORITHM 2:

A second approach depends upon whether n is zero, positive and odd, or positive and even. Division operator / denotes integer division which provides integer part of the result.

$$a^n = 1, \qquad\qquad \text{if } n \text{ is zero,}$$
$$a^n = a * a^{n/2} * a^{n/2}, \qquad\qquad \text{if } n \text{ is positive and odd,}$$
$$a^n = a^{n/2} * a^{n/2}, \qquad\qquad \text{if } n \text{ is positive and even.}$$

```
// PRECONDITIONS: n is nonnegative integer, a is a number of type double, not both are
// zero.
double power2(double a, int n)
{
   if (n == 0)
      return 1.0;
   else if (n % 2 == 1)                          // n odd
      return a * power2(a, n/2) * power2(a, n/2);
   else                                          // n even
      return power2(a, n/2) * power2(a, n/2);
}
```

ALGORITHM 3:

Algorithm 3 is an efficient modification of Algorithm 2. It uses the same recursive definition as Algorithm 2, but it is implemented by invoking only one recursive subproblem by storing the result in a variable to be multiplied by itself (squared). Of the three algorithms this is the best one. It works in logarithmic time.

```
// PRECONDITIONS: n nonnegative integer, a is of type double, a and n are not both zero.
double power3(double a, int n)
{
    int temp;
    if (n == 0)
      return 1.0;
    else
    {
        temp = power3(a, n/2);
        if (n % 2 == 1)                // n odd
          return a * temp * temp);
        else                           // n even
          return temp * temp;
    }
}
```

 7) Write a method to count the number of digits in an integer value *n*. Assume that *n* is nonnegative and represented in base ten.

ALGORITHM:

When the number is less than or equal to 9, one can discern the answer without referring to a subproblem. Such a number has just one digit. Otherwise, call subproblem to obtain the number digits in the number which has same digits as n without the last one, then finally add one to account for the last digit.

```
// PRECONDITION: n nonnegative integer
int numberOfDigits(int n)
{
    if (n <= 9)
        return 1;
    else
        return 1 + numberOfDigits(n / 10);
}
```

 8) Write a boolean method that will determine whether or not a nonnegative integer *n* contains the numeral *k*, where *k* is in the range $0 \le k \le 9$.

ALGORITHM:

Use remainder and division operations to isolate last digit, and number n without last digit. For the base cases, when $0 \le n \le 9$, n has only one digit, one asks whether n equals k, and otherwise, one asks if the rightmost digit of n equals k. Depending on the result in these cases, either `true` or `false` will be returned. The recursive case calls the method with the quotient of n upon division by 10 (the remaining digits), and the target value, k.

```
// PRECONDITIONS: n nonnegative integer,  k one digit nonnegative integer
boolean nContainsK(int n, int k)
{
    if (n<=9)
        return n == k;
    else if (n % 10 == k)
        return true;
    else
        return nContainsK(n/10, k);
}
```

 9) Write a method to compute the greatest common divisor, GCD, of two integer values m and n, such that m and n are nonnegative and not both are zero.

ALGORITHM:

The greatest common divisor, GCD, of two integer values, m and n, is the largest number which (evenly) divides both m and n. The function, GCD, is recursively defined as follows:

$$GCD(m, n) = n \qquad \text{if } n \text{ is a divisor of } m,$$
$$GCD(m, n) = GCD(n, m\%n) \qquad \text{otherwise.}$$

```
// PRECONDITIONS: m, n nonnegative
int gcd(int m, int n)
{
    if (n == 0)
        return m;
    else
        return gcd(n, m % n);
}
```

 10) Given a positive integer value n, write a method to compute the sum of the first n integers $1 + 2 + 3 + \ldots + n$.

ALGORITHM:

If *n* is one, return one. Otherwise, the sum of the first *n* nonnegative integers is the sum of value *n* plus the sum of the first *n*-1 integers.

```
// PRECONDITION: n positive integer
int nSum(int n)
{
    if (n == 1)
       return 1;
    else
       return n + nSum(n-1);
}
```

 11) Given a positive integer value *n*, write a method to compute the sum of the squares of the first *n* integers $1^2 + 2^2 + 3^2 + \ldots + n^2$.

ALGORITHM:

If *n* is one, return one. Otherwise, the sum of the first *n* squares is the sum of value n^2 plus the sum of the first *n*-1 squares.

```
// PRECONDITION: n positive integer
int sumSquares(int n)
{
    if (n == 1)
       return 1;
    else
       return n*n + sumSquares(n-1);
}
```

 12) Given a positive integer value *n*, write a method to compute the sum of the cubes of the first *n* integers $1^3 + 2^3 + 3^3 + \ldots + n^3$.

ALGORITHM:

If *n* is one, return one. Otherwise, the sum of the first *n* cubes is the sum of the value n^3 plus the sum of the first *n*-1 cubes.

```
// PRECONDITION: n positive integer
int sumCubes(int n)
{
```

```
      if (n == 1)
         return 1;
      else
         return n*n*n + sumCubes(n-1);
}
```

 13) Given a positive integer value *n*, write a method to compute the sum of the reciprocal values of the first *n* integers $1/1 + 1/2 + 1/3 + \ldots + 1/n$.

ALGORITHM:

If *n* is one, return 1. Otherwise, return the sum of 1 over *n* plus the sum of the first *n*-1 reciprocals.

```
// PRECONDITION: n positive integer
double invnSum(int n)
{
    if (n == 1)
       return 1.0;
    else
       return 1.0 / n + invnSum(n-1);
}
```

 14) Given a positive integer value *n*, write a method to compute the sum of the reciprocal values of the squares of the first *n* terms $1/1^2 + 1/2^2 + 1/3^2 + \ldots + 1/n^2$.

ALGORITHM:

If *n* is one, return 1. Otherwise, return the sum of 1 over the square of *n* plus the sum of the first *n*-1 reciprocals of squares.

```
// PRECONDITION: n positive integer
double invnSquareSum(int n)
{
    if (n == 1)
       return 1.0;
    else
       return 1.0 / (n * n) + invnSquareSum(n-1);
}
```

15) Given a positive integer value *n,* write a method to compute the sum of the reciprocal values of the factorials $1/1! + 1/2! + 1/3! + \ldots + 1/n!$.

ALGORITHM:

When *n* is one, return 1. Otherwise, return the sum of 1 over the factorial of *n* plus the sum of the first *n*-1 reciprocals of factorials.

```
// PRECONDITION: n nonnegative integer
double invFacSum(int n)
{
    if (n == 1)
        return 1.0;
    else
        return 1.0 / factorial(n) + invFacSum(n-1);
}
```

 16) Given a positive integer value *n*, write a method to compute the sum of the reciprocal values of cubes $1/1^3 + 1/2^3 + 1/3^3 + \ldots + 1/n^3$.

ALGORITHM:

When *n* is one, return 1. Otherwise, return the sum of 1 over the cube of *n* plus the sum of the reciprocals of the first *n*-1 cubes.

```
// PRECONDITION: n positive integer
double invCubesSum(int n)
{
    if (n == 1)
        return 1.0;
    else
        return 1.0 / (n*n*n) + invCubesSum(n-1);
}
```

 17) Given a positive integer value *n*, and a real value *x*, write a method to compute the sum of the first *n* terms of the series $1/x + 1/2x^2 + 1/3x^3 + \ldots + 1/nx^n$.

ALGORITHM:

When *n* is one, return $1/x$. Otherwise, return 1 over the product of *n* and the value of *x* raised to the power of *n* plus the result of the subproblem, the sum of the first *n*-1 terms in the series.

```
// PRECONDITION: n positive integer, x a number of type double
// Use method power3 defined in example 6) to get x^n.
double sumInvPow(int n, double x)
{
    if (n == 1)
      return 1.0 / x;
    else
      return 1.0 / (n * power3(x, n)) + sumInvPow(n-1, x);
}
```

 18) Write a method to compute the *n*-th number in the Lucas sequence. This sequence is constructed in the same manner as the Fibonacci sequence, with the difference that the two initial values are 1 and 3.

The Lucas numbers are named after the mathematician François Édouard Anatole Lucas, who studied both that sequence and the closely related Fibonacci numbers that we discussed in the introduction.

ALGORITHM:

There are two base cases. If $n=1$, lucas returns 1; if n equals 2, lucas returns 3; and otherwise, it returns the sum of lucas($n-1$) and lucas($n-2$).

```
// PRECONDITION: n positive integer
int lucas(int n)
{
    if (n == 1)
      return 1;
    else if (n == 2)
      return 3;
    else
      return lucas(n-1) + lucas(n-2);
}
```

 19) For given nonnegative integers *m* and *n*, write code to return Ackermann's function of *m* and *n*. Ackermann's function is defined as follows:

$$Ack(0, n) = n + 1 \qquad \text{for } m = 0$$
$$Ack(m, 0) = Ack(m - 1, 1) \qquad \text{for } m > 0 \text{ and } n = 0$$
$$Ack(m, n) = Ack(m - 1, Ack(m, n - 1)) \qquad \text{for } m > 0 \text{ and } n > 0$$

ALGORITHM:

Algorithm is straightforward from the definition. Computation of this function grows exponentially. Test this with small values of *m* and *n*. It grows even faster than an exponential algorithm.

```
// PRECONDITIONS: m nonnegative integer, n nonnegative integer, not both zero.
int ack(int m, int n)
{
    if (m == 0)
        return n+1;
    else if ((m > 0) && (n == 0))
        return ack(m-1, 1);
    else if ((m > 0) && (n > 0))
        return ack(m-1, ack(m, n-1));
}
```

 20) Write a method to display the digits of a given integer value *n* in reverse order.

ALGORITHM:

Isolate each digit from right to left. One way to do this is to obtain the remainder upon division of *n* by 10, print it out and invoke the recursive subproblem with *n* divided by 10.

```
// PRECONDITION: n nonnegative integer
void printReverse(int n)
{
    System.out.print(n % 10);  // display last digit first
    if (n <= 9)                // n has one digit
        System.out.println();
    else
        printReverse(n / 10);
}
```

 21) Write a method to determine whether or not the digits of a given nonnegative number *n* form a palindrome. (Hint: Use the method that returns the number of digits from example 7.)

ALGORITHM:

Each nonnegative number smaller than or equal to 9 is a palindrome. If the first and the last digits of *n* are not the same, return `false`; otherwise, the answer is the same as when we use the original number without the first and the last digits in it as the parameter *n*.

```
// PRECONDITION: n nonnegative of type long, numberOfDigits number of digits of n
boolean isPalindrome(long n, int numberOfDigits)
{
    long first, last;
    if (numberOfDigits <= 1)
      return true;                    //A number with only one digit is a palindrome.
    else

    {
        first = (long)(n / power1(10.0, numberOfDigits - 1));
        last = n % 10;                // obtain first and last digit
        if (first != last)
            return false;
        else                          // first and last digit the same
            return isPalindrome((long)(n % power1(10,
                    numberOfDigits - 1) / 10), numberOfDigits - 2);
    }
}
```

 22) Write a method to calculate the binomial coefficients for the integer values n and k, such that n and k are nonnegative and k is less than or equal to n, i.e., they satisfy the property $0 <= k <= n$.

Row 0:					1				
Row 1:				1		1			
Row 2:			1		2		1		
Row 3:		1		3		3		1	
Row 4:	1		4		6		4		1

ALGORITHM:

Given $0 \le k \le n$, *binomial(n,k)* determines the number of unique ways in which k objects can be chosen from a collection of n objects. Value n choose k can be determined from Pascal's triangle where n is the row number and k is the position in the row starting from zero. For example, value 6 is *binomial(4,2)*. When n equals 0, or when n equals k, the method returns 1; otherwise, it returns the sum of *binomial(n-1, k)* and *binomial(n-1, k-1)*.

```
// PRECONDITIONS:  n>=k, and k>=0
int binomial(int n, int k)
{
```

```
    if ((k == 0) || (n == k))
        return 1;
    else
        return binomial(n-1, k-1) + binomial(n-1, k);
}
```

 23) Write a method to convert a nonnegative number *n*, represented in base 10 (decimal), to base 2 (binary) notation.

ALGORITHM:

If *n* is less than or equal to 1, print *n*; otherwise, apply the same method recursively with the parameter *n/2*, and, after that, print the remainder upon dividing *n* by 2.

```
// PRECONDITION: n nonnegative integer
void convert(int n)
{
    if (n <= 1)
        System.out.println(n);
    else
    {
        convert(n / 2);
        System.out.print(n % 2);
    }
}
```

 24) Write a method to convert a positive number $n \geq 3$ in base 10 to another base *b* notation. Assume that $n > b \geq 2$.

ALGORITHM:

The process of converting any number represented in base 10 to another base *b* may use a similar algorithm as in the example above, except that the division is by the value of *b*.

```
// PRECONDITION:  n > b >= 2
void convert_n_b(int n, int b)
{
    if (n > 0)
    {
        convert_n_b(n / b, b);
```

```
        System.out.print(n % b);
    }
}
```

 25) Write a method to return a string of digits corresponding to a nonnegative number *n* converted from base 10 to base 3 notation.

ALGORITHM:

The process of converting any number represented in base 10 to base 3 may use a similar algorithm as in the example above, except that the division is by the value of 3.

```
// PRECONDITION: n >= 0
String convertToBase3(int n)
{
    String result = "";
    if (n < 3)
        result += n;
    else
        result = convertToBase3(n/3) + n%3;
    return result;
}
```

 26) For a nonnegative integer *n* write a method to determine the number of digits for *n*'s base two representation (or *n*'s binary format).

ALGORITHM:

If the number is 0 or1 return 1. Otherwise, return one more than the number of digits returned by calling the subproblem for *n*/2.

```
// PRECONDITION: n >= 0
int numberOfDigits(int n)
{
    if (n <= 1)
        return 1;
    else
        return 1 + numberOfDigits(n/2);
}
```

27) Given a nonnegative integer n, write a method that prints the letter "A" $\log_2(n)$ times. Test it with numbers n of the type 2^n.

ALGORITHM:

If n is 0, do nothing. Otherwise, call the subproblem for $n/2$, and print one letter "A".

```
// PRECONDITION:  n >= 0
void printAlognTimes(int n)
{
    if (n >= 1)
    {
        printAlognTimes(n/2);
        System.out.println("A");
    }
}
```

 28) Write a method to display a nonnegative integer of type long with commas in the appropriate locations. For example, for $n = 31245$, it should display 31,245, and, for $n = 10000$, it displays 10,000.

ALGORITHM:

If n is less than 1,000, print that number. Otherwise, apply the same method recursively to the quotient upon dividing the number, n, by 1000. After that, print commas as needed.

```
// PRECONDITION: n nonnegative integer of type long
void printCommas(long n)
{
    if (n < 1000)
        System.out.print(n);
    else
    {
        printCommas(n / 1000);
        System.out.print(",");
        if ((n % 1000) < 10)
        {
            System.out.print("00");
            System.out.print(n % 1000);
        }
        else if ((n % 1000) < 100)
        {
            System.out.print("0");
            System.out.print(n % 1000);
```

```
        }
        else
            System.out.print(n % 1000);
    }
}
```

 29) Given a nonnegative integer *n*, write a method that prints the letter "A" 2^n times.

ALGORITHM:

If the number *n* is 0, print one letter "A". Otherwise, call twice the recursive subproblem with parameter *n*-1 .

```
// PRECONDITION: n >= 0
void printAExpTimes(int n)
{
    if (n==0)
        System.out.println("A");
    else
    {
        printAExpTimes(n-1);
        printAExpTimes(n-1);
    }
}
```

 30) Write a method that accepts a positive integer *n* and prints *n* letter "O"s in a line. For *n* equal to 5 the line looks like OOOOO.

ALGORITHM

If *n* is one, print one "O". Otherwise, call the recursive method to print *n*-1 "O"s and after that print one additional "O" to complete the original task.

```
// PRECONDITION: n >0
void printOneLineOs(int n)
{
    if (n==1)
        System.out.print("O");
    else
    {
```

38

```
        printOneLineOs(n-1);
        System.out.print( "O");
    }
}
```

 31) Write a method that accepts a positive integer *n* and prints "O"s in a triangle of *n* lines. The first line has one "O", second line has two "O"s, and the *n*-th line has *n* "O"s. All lines are left aligned. For *n* equal to 5, the triangle looks like this:

```
O
OO
OOO
OOOO
OOOOO
```

ALGORITHM:

If *n* is one, print one "O" and move to a new line. Otherwise, call the recursive method to print the triangle with *n*-1 lines of "O"s and after that, print one additional line of *n* "O"s to complete the original task.

```
// PRECONDITION: n >0
void printTriangle(int n)
{
    if (n==1)
    {
        System.out.print("O");        // print one O
        System.out.println("");        // move to a new line
    }
    else if (n>1)
    {
        printTriangle(n-1);            // print a triangle with n-1 lines
        printOneLineOs(n);             // print one line with n letters O
        System.out.println();          // move to a new line
    }
}
```

 32) Write a method that accepts a positive integer *n* and prints "O"s in a triangle of *n* lines. The first line has *n* "O"s, second line has *n*-1 "O"s, and the *n*-th line has one "O". All lines are left aligned. For *n* equal to 5 the upside down triangle looks like:

```
OOOOO
OOOO
OOO
OO
O
```

ALGORITHM

If *n* is one, print one "O" and move to a new line. Otherwise, print one line of *n* "O"s, move to a new line, and call the recursive method to print the upside down triangle with *n*-1 lines of "O"s to complete the original task.

```
// PRECONDITION: n >0
void printTriangleUpsideDown(int n)
{
   if (n==1)
   {
      System.out.print("O");
      System.out.println();
   }
   else if (n>1)
   {
      printOneLineOs(n);
      System.out.println();
      printTriangleUpsideDown(n-1);
   }
}
```

33) Write a method that accepts an initial *balance*, percentage of yearly interest *rate*, and number *n* of months for CD to become available for withdrawal, and returns resulting CD balance after *n* months. Interest added after each month equals to (*balance* * *rate* *0.01/12).

```
public double resultCD (double balance, double r, int month)
{
     if (month <= 0)
       return balance;
     else
     {
        balance = balance + balance * r * 0.01 / 12;
        return resultCD (balance, r, month - 1 );
     }
}
```

34) Write a method that accepts initial *balance*, yearly interest *rate*, and *year* which is equal to 0 when method is invoked. Year is increment after each year of saving passes. Method returns number of years needed to keep saving, without any withdrawal, until balance reaches or exceeds one million dollars.

```
public int yearsToMillion(double balance, double rate, int
                          year)
{
    if (balance > 1000000)
        return 0;
    else
        return yearsToMillion(balance*(1 + rate*0.01), rate,
                              year+1);
}
```

35) Write a method that accepts initial *balance*, yearly interest *rate*, and *year* which is equal to 0 when method is invoked. Year is incremented after each year of saving passes. Interest as added yearly. Method should display balance after each year of saving until balance reaches or exceeds one million dollars.

```
public void yearlyBalanceToBecomeMillionaire(double balance,
                                         double rate, int year)
{
    if (balance < 1000000)
    {
        balance = balance + balance*rate/100;
        year++;
        System.out.print("$"+(int)(balance + 0.5));
        System.out.println ("\t" + year);
        yearlyBalanceToBecomeMillionaire(balance, rate, year);
    }
}
```

36) Given a positive integer value *n*, write a method that prints the letter "A" *n*! times. Call the subproblem for *n*-1 *n* times.

ALGORITHM: If the number *n* is 1, print one letter "A". Otherwise, use a loop to iterate *n* times and at each iteration call one recursive subproblem with the argument *n*-1 (Very small values should be used for *n* to test how it works). This is one of the fastest growing algorithms.

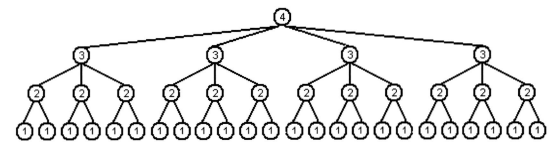

Let us illustrate the trace of recursive calls for the invocation `printAFactorialTimes(4)`. The tree of recursive calls has nodes that only specify actual parameters when the recursive subproblems are called. Each recursive call of `printAFactorialTimes(1)` prints one letter "A". So, there will be 24 or 4! letter "A"s printed.

```
// PRECONDITION: n > 0
void printAFactorialTimes(int n)
{
    if (n == 1)
        System.out.println("A");
    else
    {
        for (int i=1; i<=n, i++)
            printAFactorialTimes(n-1);
    }
}
```

 37) Write a method that accepts a one digit positive integer *n* and returns an ArrayList of all permutations of the numbers 1, 2, 3, …, *n*.

ALGORITHM:

If *n* equals 1, return the ArrayList with the string "1" as its only element. For *n*>1, generate all permutations of first *n*-1 numbers. Each such permutation is a string of length *n*-1. For each permutation create *n* new permutations by inserting *n* at the beginning, between every two consecutive characters, and after the end of the string.

```
// PRECONDITION: n >0
ArrayList<String> permutations(int n)
{
    ArrayList<String> result, oldResult;
    String current;
```

42

```
    result = new ArrayList<String>();
    if(n == 1)
    {
        result.add("1");
        return result;
    }
    else
    {
        oldResult = permutations(n-1);  // get all permutations of n-1 elements
        for(String oldCurrent: oldResult)
        {
            result.add(n + oldCurrent);
            for(int j = 0; j<n-1; j++)
            {
                current = oldCurrent.substring(0,j+1) + n +
                          oldCurrent.substring(j+1,n-1 );
                result.add(current);
            }
        }
        return result;
    }
}
```

 38) Write a method that accepts a one digit positive integer *n* and returns an ArrayList of all subsets of the set {1, 2, 3, ..., *n*}. Denote the empty set as "0".

ALGORITHM:

If *n* equals 0, return the ArrayList with the string "0" (denoting an empty set) as its only element. For *n*>0, generate all subsets of the first *n*-1 numbers. Add each such subset to the resulting ArrayList. In addition, include a number *n* in each subset of all the subsets of the first *n*-1 numbers and also add it to the resulting ArrayList.

```
// PRECONDITION: n >0
ArrayList<String> powerSet(int n)
{
    ArrayList<String> result, oldResult;
    String current;
    result = new ArrayList<String>();
    if(n == 0)
      result.add("0");
    else
    {
```

```
         oldResult = powerSet(n-1);
         for(String oldCurrent: oldResult)
            result.add(oldCurrent);

         for(String oldCurrent: oldResult)
            if (oldCurrent != "0")
               result.add(oldCurrent+", " + n);
            else
               result.add("" + n);
      }
      return result;
}
```

In the remaining examples in this chapter the code for recursive method is given, and outcome should be determined without running the code. When outcome for one specific value of n has to be determined, the best is to trace the execution, as shown in the introduction. When outcome should be determined for consecutive values of n the result for n-1 can be reused to determine the outcome for n.

  39)   Determine the outcome of the following code when invoked with the specified values 1… 5 of the input parameter n.

```
//PRECONDITION: n positive
int mystery1(int n)
{
   if (n == 1)
      return 1;
   else
      return n + mystery1(n-1);
}
```

```
//PRECONDITION: n positive or zero
int mystery2(int n)
{
   if (n == 0)
      return 1;
   else
      return n + mystery1(n-1);
}
```

ANSWERS:

n	1	2	3	4	5
mystery1(n)	1	3	6	10	15
mystery2(n)	2	4	7	11	16

40)   Determine the outcome of the following code when invoked with the specified values 1… 5 of the input parameter *n*.

//PRECONDITION: n positive	//PRECONDITION: n positive or zero
``int mystery3(int n)
{
if (n == 1)
return 1;
else
return n * mystery3(n-1);
}```	```int mystery4(int n)
{
if (n == 0)
return 0;
else
return n * mystery4(n-1);
}```

ANSWERS:

n	1	2	3	4	5
mystery3(n)	1	2	6	24	120
mystery4(n)	0	0	0	0	0

CHAPTER 3   EXAMPLES ON ARRAYS

Recursive methods with an array and its actual size as parameters

Examples include: determine the largest element in an array, test if array is sorted, apply insertion sort, selection sort, bubble sort, test if it is a palindrome, perform binary and ternary search, and similar

Most methods within this section have been designed for a given array named *list* storing *n* integers. We work with arrays of integer type first because arithmetic operations and comparison of elements are simpler. In this way, learners need only concentrate on writing code recursively. Parameter n is the array's actual size, and must be less than or equal to *list.length* since the number of stored data cannot exceed the declared array's size. Indices in an array start at zero; therefore, an array with *n* elements will have those elements stored at positions 0, 1, ..., *n*-1.

Obviously, with minor modifications as shown at the end of this chapter, any example can be modified to be defined for an array of any desired type of objects. The last three examples in this section are defined for an array of String type, an array of Student type and an array of Comparable type, respectively.

EXAMPLES

1)   Write a method to print all the elements of the nonempty array, *list*, of size *n*.

ALGORITHM:

As long as *n* is positive, the method is called recursively for the subarray of size *n*-1, and then the last element is printed.

```
//PRECONDITIONS: array is nonempty, n is positive
void printArray (int[] list, int n)
{
   if (n > 0)
   {
      printArray (list, n-1);
      System.out.print(list[n-1] + " ");
   }
}
```

2) Write a method to print all the elements of the nonempty array, *list*, of size *n*, in reverse order.

ALGORITHM:

As long as *n* is positive, the last element is printed and then the recursive method is called for the subarray of size *n*-1.

```
//PRECONDITIONS: array is nonempty, n is positive
void printArrayReversed(int[] list, int n)
{
  if (n > 0)
  {
     System.out.print(list[n-1] + " ");
     printArrayReversed(list, n-1);
  }
}
```

 3)   Write a method to compute the sum of all elements of the array *list*, of size *n*.

ALGORITHM:

When the array is empty, return zero; otherwise, return the sum of the subarray (all elements without the last element) plus the value of the last array element.

```
//PRECONDITIONS: array may be empty or not, n nonnegative integer
int sum(int[] list, int n)
{
   if (n == 0)
     return 0;
   else
     return list[n-1] + sum(list, n-1);
}
```

 4)   Write a method to compute the product of all elements of the nonempty array, *list*, of size *n*.

ALGORITHM:

When the array has a single element, return that element; otherwise, return the product of the last array element, multiplied by the product of all elements in the array excluding the last element.

```
// PRECONDITION: array is nonempty
int product(int[] list, int n)
{
    if (n == 1)
        return list[0];
    else
        return list[n-1] * product(list, n-1);
}
```

 5)   Write a method to count the number of elements that have the same value as the variable, *item*, in the array, *list,* of size *n*.

ALGORITHM:

When the array is empty, return zero; otherwise, if the last element in the array is equal to *item*, then we add one to our count of equal elements in the array without the last element, and, if not, just return the count of equal elements in the array without the last element.

```
//PRECONDITION: n nonnegative
int countItem(int[] list, int n, int item)
{
    if (n == 0)
        return 0;
    else if (list[n-1] == item)
        return 1 + countItem(list, n-1, item);
    else
        return countItem(list, n-1, item);
}
```

6) Write a method to determine the largest value of the nonempty array, *list*, of size *n*.

ALGORITHM:
When the array has a single element, that element is the largest; otherwise, let *temp* be the largest element in the array without the last element. If *temp* is larger than the last array element, return *temp*; otherwise, return the value of the last array element.

```
//PRECONDITION: n is positive
int maxItem(int[] list, int n)
{
    if (n == 1)
        return list[0];
```

```
    else
    {
       int temp = maxItem(list, n-1);
       if (temp > list[n-1])
         return temp;
       else
         return list[n-1];
    }
}
```

 7)   Write a method to determine the index of the element in the array, *list*, whose value is equal to a given value, *item*. Assume that there are no duplicates. If no element in *list* matches *item*, the method should return -1.

ALGORITHM:

If the array is empty, return -1. If the last element equals *item,* return *n*-1; otherwise, use the answer to the subproblem where the array has a size of *n*-1.

```
//PRECONDITIONS: array may be empty or not, n nonnegative integer
int location(int[] list, int n, int item)
{
   if (n == 0)
      return -1;
   else if (list[n-1] == item)
      return n-1;
   else
      return location(list, n-1, item);
}
```

 8)   Write a method to determine if the given value, *item*, is found in the array, *list.*

ALGORITHM:

This problem is quite similar to example 6, above. Since this problem returns a boolean value, however, we need only return a `true` or `false` value rather than the location of the element that equals the given value, *item.*

```
//PRECONDITIONS: array may be empty or not, n nonnegative integer
boolean itemIn( int[] list, int n, int item)
{
   if (n == 0)
      return false;
```

```
    else if (list[n-1] == item)
      return true;
    else
      return itemIn(list, n-1, item);
}
```

9)   Write a method to count the number of elements in the array, *list*, of size *n*, that have positive values.

ALGORITHM:

If the array is empty, return 0. Otherwise, if the last array element is positive, return one more than the number of positive elements in the subarray; however, if the last element is not positive, return the number of positive elements in the subarray. The subarray is the same as the original array, *list*, without its last element.

```
//PRECONDITIONS: array may be empty or not, n nonnegative integer
int countPositive(int[] list, int n)
{
   if (n == 0)
     return 0;
   else if (list[n-1] > 0)
     return 1 + countPositive(list, n-1);
   else
     return countPositive(list, n-1);
}
```

10) Write a method to count the number of odd elements in the array, *list*, of size *n*.

ALGORITHM:

This example is analogous to the example to count positive elements.

```
//PRECONDITIONS: array may be empty or not, n nonnegative integer
int countOdd(int[] list, int n)
{
   if (n == 0)
     return 0;
   else if (list[n-1] % 2 == 0)
     return countOdd(list, n-1);
   else
     return 1 + countOdd(list, n-1);
}
```

11) Write a method to determine whether or not two arrays, *list1* and *list2*, of sizes *n1* and *n2* respectively, are equal. Return a boolean value of `true` or of `false` based on whether or not all their corresponding elements have equal values.

ALGORITHM:

If the arrays have different sizes, then, clearly, they are not equal. Similarly, if both are empty, they are equal. As long as the corresponding elements of each array are equal, continue to recursively call the method, comparing each corresponding previous pair. As soon as an inequality is found, stop recursion and return a value of `false`.

```
//PRECONDITIONS: arrays may be empty or not, n1 and n2 nonnegative integers
boolean equalArrays(int[] list1, int[] list2, int n1, int n2)
{
    if (n1 != n2)
      return false;
    else if (n1 == 0)
      return true;
    else if (list1[n1-1] != list2[n2-1])
      return false;
    else
      return equalArrays(list1, list2, n1-1, n2-1);
}
```

 12) Write a method that will return the position of the largest element in the nonempty array, *list*, with *n* occupied positions.

ALGORITHM:

If the nonempty *list* has a single element, return 0. Otherwise, let *temp* be the location of the largest element in the subarray *list*, without its last element *list[n-1]*. Compare *list[temp]* and *list[n-1]* and return the index of the greater one.

```
//PRECONDITION: array is nonempty
int maxIndex(int[] list, int n)
{
    if (n == 1)
      return 0;
    else
    {
      int temp = maxIndex(list, n-1);
      if (list[temp] > list[n-1])
```

```
            return temp;
        else
            return n-1;
    }
}
```

13) Write a method to change the array, *list*, in such a way that each element has double the value that it had previously.

ALGORITHM:

If the array is empty, there is nothing to be done. Otherwise, double the value of *list[n-1]* and then perform the same for the subarray (as defined in the previous example).

```
//PRECONDITIONS: array may be empty or not, n nonnegative integer
void doubleArrayValues(int[] list, int n)
{
    if (n > 0)
    {
      list[n-1] = 2 * list[n-1];
      if (n > 1)
        doubleArrayValues(list, n-1);
    }
}
```

14) Write a method to print all of the elements of the array, *list*, from the given positions *first* to *last*. Have them printed in the same order as they appear in the array.

ALGORITHM:

Since we need to print all elements in the order in which they are stored in the array, we have to begin with the first element. We print the value of each successive element in the array for as long as our *first* index is less than or equal to our *last* index. At this point, recursion stops, and control returns, resolving all previous calls.

```
//PRECONDITIONS: first >= 0 , last < n, first <= last
//array is nonempty
void printSubarray(int[] list, int n, int first, int last)
{
    if (first <= last)
    {
```

```
        System.out.println(list[first] + " ");
        printSubarray(list, n, first+1, last);
    }
}
```

 15) Write a method to determine whether or not a given one-dimensional array, *list*, with *n* integer values, is sorted in ascending (increasing) order. The method should return the boolean value `true` if the array elements are sorted in increasing order, and `false` otherwise.

ALGORITHM:

If the size of the array is less than or equal to 1, then return `true`; otherwise, if the value of the last element is greater than or equal to the element that precedes it, test if the array elements without the last element are increasing. Finally, return `false` if the value of the last array element is less than the element that precedes it.

```
//PRECONDITION: array is nonempty
boolean increasing(int[] list, int n)
{
    if (n <= 1)
        return true;
    else if (list[n-1] >= list[n-2])
        return increasing(list, n-1);
    else
        return false;
}
```

 16) Write a method to assign the elements of the nonempty array, *list*, of size *n*, values: 1, 2, 3, …, *n*.

ALGORITHM:

If the array contains only one element, store a value of one in that element. When *n* is greater than one, the task will be completed if we call the subproblem of size *n*-1 recursively, assigning the first *n*-1 elements values of 1, 2, 3, …, (*n*-1), and after that assign *n* to the last element.

```
//PRECONDITIONS: array is nonempty, n is positive
void assign1ton(int[] list, int n)
{
    if (n == 1)
```

```
      list[0]=1;
   else if (n > 1)
   {
      assign1ton(list, n-1);
      list[n-1] = n;
   }
}
```

 17) Write a method to assign the elements of the nonempty array, *list*, of size *n,* values: $1, 2, 4, 8, \ldots, 2^n$.

ALGORITHM:

If the array contains only one element, store the value one in that element. When *n* is greater than one, the task will be completed if we call the subproblem of size *n*-1 recursively, assigning the first *n*-1 elements values of $1, 2, 4, 8, \ldots, 2^{n-1}$, followed by assigning twice the value of the second to last element to the last element in the array.

```
//PRECONDITION: array is not empty, n positive integer
void assignPowersOfTwo(int[] list, int n)
{
   if (n == 1)
      list[0]=1;
   else if (n > 1)
   {
      assignPowersOfTwo(list, n-1);
      list[n-1] = 2*list[n-2];
   }
}
```

 18) Write a method to sort the elements of the array, *list*, of size *n*, by applying the selection sort algorithm.

ALGORITHM:

If the array is empty or contains only one element, there is nothing to do. Such arrays are sorted. When *n* is greater than one, swap the largest element with the element at the last place in the array; after that, sort the first *n*-1 elements recursively.

```
//PRECONDITION: array may be empty or not, n nonnegative integer
void selectionSort(int[] list, int n)
{
```

```
   int indexMax, temp;
   if (n > 1)
   {
      indexMax = 0;
      for ( int i=1; i<=n-1; i++)    // find the index of the largest element
         if (list[i]>list[indexMax])
            indexMax = i;
      temp = list[n-1];                    //swap the largest and the last element
      list[n-1] = list[indexMax];
      list[indexMax] = temp;
      selectionSort(list, n-1);        // sort subarray of n-1 elements recursively
   }
}
```

 19) Write a method to sort the array, *list*, of size *n*, by applying the insertion sort.

ALGORITHM:

If the array is empty or contains only one element, there is nothing to do. Such arrays are sorted. When *n* is greater than one, sort the first *n*-1 elements recursively; after that, insert the last element, *list[n-1]*, into the sorted subarray.

```
//PRECONDITION: array may be empty or not, n nonnegative integer
void insertionSort(int[] list, int n)
{
   int i, temp;
   if (n > 1)
   {
      insertionSort(list, n-1);             // sort the first n-1elements
      temp = list[n-1];
      i = n-1;
      while (i>0 && list[n-1]> temp)    // insert list[n-1] into the sorted subarray
      {
         list[i] = list[i-1];
         i--;
      }
      list[i] = temp;
   }
}
```

20) Write a method to sort the elements of the array, *list*, of size *n*, by applying the bubble sort algorithm.

ALGORITHM:

If *n* is 0 or 1, nothing needs to be done. If the size of the array is larger than one, put the largest element at the last position in the array by swapping every two consecutive elements in the array that are out of order (larger value before the smaller one). Next, recursively sort the sublist of the first *n*-1 elements.

```
//PRECONDITION: array may be empty or not, n nonnegative integer
void bubbleSort(int[] list, int n)
{ int i, temp;
  if (n > 1)
  {
    for(i=0; i<n-1; i++)
       if (list[i] > list[i+1])
       {
           temp = list[i];
           list[i] = list[i+1];
           list[i+1] = temp;
       }
    bubbleSort(list, n-1);
  }
}
```

 21) Write a method to return `true` if the elements of the nonempty array, *numbers*, an array that only stores single digit integers, make a palindrome; otherwise, return the value `false`.

ALGORITHM:

If the array's size is 0 or 1, the array is a palindrome, so return `true`. If the size of the array is larger than one, check if the first and last elements are the same. If they are not the same, return `false`; otherwise, return the same answer as the call to the subproblem that contains the array without the first and last elements. (Note: Call the method by passing *numbers*, 0, and *n*-1 for the formal parameters *numbers*, *first*, and *last*, respectively. The number of elements is *last-first+1*.)

```
//PRECONDITION: array is nonempty, last>=first>=0
boolean isPalindrome(int[] numbers, int first, int last)
{
   if (first>=last)
     return true;
```

```
    else if ( numbers[first] != numbers[last])
      return false;
    else
      return isPalindrome(numbers, first+1, last-1);
}
```

 22) Write a method to perform a binary search on a nonempty array. The method accepts an integer array named *list*, a value, *key*, that we are searching for, and *first* and *last* denoting the indices for the subarray of the array, *list*, where we currently search for the key. The method returns the index in the array where *key* was found; it returns -1 if *key* is not found.

ALGORITHM:

The key cannot be found in an empty list. So, when *first* is greater than *last* return -1. Otherwise, if *key* is equal to the array element at position *mid*, the middle of that array, return *mid*. If *key* is different from *list[mid]*, it is either smaller or larger than *list[mid]*. Since list is sorted, we need only further search in one half of the array. If *key<list[mid]*, we recursively call *binarySearch* with the subarray portion between *first* and *mid* - 1; otherwise, we recursively call *binarySearch* with the subarray portion of the list between *mid* + 1 and *last*.

```
//PRECONDITION: array is nonempty, last>=first>=0
int binarySearch(int[] list, int first, int last, int key)
{
    if (first > last)
        return -1;
    else
    {
       int mid = (first + last)/2;
       if (key == list[mid])
          return mid;
       else if (key < list[mid])
          return binarySearch(list, first, mid-1, key);
       else
          return binarySearch(list, mid+1, last, key);
    }
}
```

23) Write a method to perform a ternary search on an array. The method accepts *key*, a key value we are searching for, *list*, an array of integers, and *first* and *last*, denoting the subarray. The method returns an integer which is the index in the array where *key* was found. In case of an unsuccessful search, the method returns a sentinel value of -1.

ALGORITHM:

Same as binary search, but now we divide into three thirds.

```
//PRECONDITION: array is nonempty, last>=first>=0
int ternarySearch(int[] list, int key, int first, int last)
{
    int pos1, pos2;
    if(first > last)
        return -1;
    pos1 = first + (last - first) / 3;
    pos2 = first + 2 * (last - first) / 3;
    if(list[pos1] == key)
        return pos1;
    else if(list[pos2] == key)
        return pos2;
    else if(key < list[pos1])
        return ternarySearch(list, key, first, pos1 - 1);
    else if(key < list[pos2])
        return ternarySearch(list, key, pos1 + 1, pos2 - 1);
    else
        return ternarySearch(list, key, pos2 + 1, last);
}
```

24) Write a method to count the number of elements that have the same value as the String variable, *item*, in the String array, *list,* of size *n*.

ALGORITHM:

When the array is empty, return zero; otherwise, if the last element in the array is equal to *item*, then we add one to our count of equal elements in the array without the last element, and, if not, just return the count of equal elements in the array without the last element.

```
//PRECONDITION: n nonnegative
int countStringItem(String[] list, int n, String item)
{
    if (n == 0)
        return 0;
```

```
     else if (list[n-1].equals(item))
       return 1 + countStringItem(list, n-1, item);
     else
       return countStringItem(list, n-1, item);
}
```

 25) Assume that the class *Student* is given and that it has the public method *isHonors()* that returns true for an honors student and false otherwise. Write a method to return the number of honors students in an array, *list*, of *Student* type and size *n*.

ALGORITHM:

Similar to *countOdd*, except that we test if the last element is an honors student instead of checking whether or not it is odd.

```
//PRECONDITION: array may be empty or not, n nonnegative integer
int countHonorsStudents(Student[] list, int n)
{
   if (n == 0)
      return 0;
   else if (list[n-1].isHonors())
      return 1+ countHonorsStudents (list, n-1);
   else
      return countHonorsStudents (list, n-1);
}
```

 26) Revise example 17 to sort the array, *list*, of type Comparable and size *n*, by applying the recursive selection sort algorithm.

NOTE: Interface Comparable is a part of Java language. It only has one method, compareTo(Object obj). Any class that implements interface Comparable must have that method implemented. When the formal parameter is an array of interface type, the actual parameter used when the method is invoked must be an array of objects from any class that implements the interface Comparable. This version of selection sort is far more general and can sort arrays of any object type as long as its class implements the Comparable interface, and, consequently, provides code that determines the way to compare array elements.

ALGORITHM:

Problem 17 and this one use the same selection sort algorithm. The difference is that variables *list* and *temp* are now of type Comparable, and that two elements in the array are compared by using the method compareTo().

```
//PRECONDITION: array may be empty or not, n nonnegative integer
void selectionSort(Comparable[] list, int n)
{
   int indexMax;
   Comparable temp;
   if (n > 1)
   {
     indexMax = 0;
     for ( int i=1; i<n; i++)            // find the index of the largest element
        if (list[i].compareTo(list[indexMax])>0)
           indexMax = i;

     temp = list[n-1];                  //swap the largest and the last element
     list[n-1] = list[indexMax];
     list[indexMax] = temp;
     selectionSort(list, n-1);          // sort list of n-1 elements
   }
}
```

CHAPTER 4   EXAMPLES ON LINKED LISTS

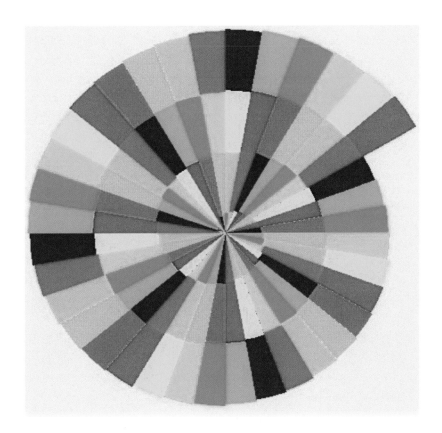

Recursive methods dealing with linked lists

Examples include: count list nodes, return reference to node with smallest data, test if nodes have data sorted in ascending order, print list data, and similar.

This chapter includes examples that perform different tasks on a given linked list. For each problem below, we write a recursive method to return the required value or perform the specified task. The base case is usually when the linked list is empty, or when the list has a single node, or both of the above. The base case specifies the answer for the task explicitly without referring to the subproblem. The recursive step defines how to solve the task on the linked list by using the solution for one or more sublists. The sublist typically starts from the successor of the first node.

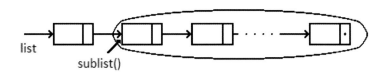

The examples in this section will use three types of assumptions specified in sections 4.1 through 4.3. Each of the three approaches have the following in common. Class Node describes a node in the linked list. Class Node has variables data and next that define the data stored and a reference to the next node in the linked list. Class LinkedList describes the linked list. The only instance variable in the class LinkedList is the variable list of Node type. All recursive methods are defined in the LinkedList class. Another possibility, not discussed here, would be to define another class that inherits from class LinkedList, and put all recursive methods into that class.

4.1 Public Node class storing int data

Section 4.1 defines the class Node as a separate public class with private instance variables, data and next, and provides public accessor and mutator methods for both variables. Variable data, in class Node, is of int type. Since primitive types can be compared with relational operators <,<=, >, >=, ==, and !=, learners have to concentrate only on writing methods recursively. Class LinkedList has an overloaded constructor. LinkedList(int number) creates a linked list with the specified `number` of nodes, with random one digit integer values. `LinkedList(Node first)` creates a linked list that is referred to by `first`. Method `sublist()` returns the linked list that starts from the second node in the original list. Method `firstNodeData()` returns the `int` data stored in the first node.

Examples 1 through 22 are defined for classes `Node`, `LinkedList`, and `TestLinkedList` as specified next. The class that contains the main method is used to test the recursive methods.

```java
public class Node
{
   private int data;
   private Node next;

   public Node()
   {
      next = null;
      data = 0;
   }

   public Node(int data)
   {
      this.data = data;
      next = null;
   }

   public Node(int data, Node next)
   {
      this.data = data;
      this.next = next;
   }

   public int getData()
   {
      return data;
   }

   public Node getNext()
   {
      return next;
   }

   public void setData(int data)
   {
      this.data = data;
```

```
        }

    public void setNext(Node next)
    {
        this.next = next;
    }
} // end class Node
```

```
import java.util.Random;

public class LinkedList
{
    private Node list;


    // Constructor creates linked list of random size with random one digit integer data values.
    // Parameter size must be nonnegative.
    public LinkedList(int size)
    {
        if (size == 0)
        {
            list = null;
        }
        else
        {
            Node curr;
            list = null;
            Random r = new Random();
            for (int i=1; i<=size; i++)
            {
                curr = new Node (Math.abs(r.nextInt()) % 10, list);
                list = curr;
            }
        }
    }

    // Constructor creates linked list that starts with node
    public LinkedList (Node node)
    {
        list = node;
    }
```

```
  // PRECONDITION: nonempty linked list
  // Returns sublist that starts from the successor of the first node.
  public LinkedList sublist()
  {
    LinkedList l = new LinkedList(list.getNext());
    return l;
  }

  // Returns data value in the first node in nonempty linked list.
  public int firstNodeData()
  {
    return list.getData();
  }

  // Returns the reference to the first node in the linked list
  public Node getFirst()
  {
    return list;
  }

  public boolean isEmpty()
  {
    return (list == null);
  }

  ///////////////////////////////////////////////////////////////////////////////////
  //
  //  insert recursive methods specified in exercises 1) – 23)  here
  //
  ///////////////////////////////////////////////////////////////////////////////////
}// end class LinkedList
```

```
public class TestLinkedList
{
  public static void main(String[] args)
  {
    LinkedList myList = new LinkedList(3);
    System.out.print("\nLinked list with 3 random integers:");
    myList.traverse();
    System.out.print("Number of nodes in the linked list: " +
                      myList.countNodes());
```

```
        System.out.print("\nList is sorted in ascending order: " +
                          myList.isAscending());

        ///////////////////////////////////////////////////////////////////////////////////
        // Write code to test the remaining recursive methods  for examples 1) – 23)
        ///////////////////////////////////////////////////////////////////////////////////
    }
}
```

SECTION 4.1 EXAMPLES

1) Write a method to traverse the linked list.

ALGORITHM:

If the list is empty, nothing should be printed. For a nonempty list, display the first node's data value, and traverse the sublist that starts from the successor of the first node.

```
public void traverse()
{
   if (list != null)
   {
      System.out.print(firstNodeData() + " ");
      sublist().traverse();
   }
   else
      System.out.println();
}
```

2) Write a method to traverse the linked list in reverse order.

ALGORITHM:

If the list is nonempty, then traverse in reverse order the sublist starting from the successor of the first node, and then display the data of the first node.

```
public void traverseReversed()
{
   if (list != null)
   {
      sublist().traverseReversed();
```

```
      System.out.println(firstNodeData() + " ");
   }
}
```

3) Write a method to return the number of nodes in a linked list.

ALGORITHM:

If the list has no nodes (i.e. it is empty), the method should return 0; otherwise, a nonempty list has one more node than the sublist that starts from the successor of the first node.

```
public int countNodes()
{
   if (list == null)
     return 0;
   else
     return 1 + sublist().countNodes();
}
```

4) Write a method to count the number of nodes in a given linked list that have the same data as a given *item*.

ALGORITHM:

This example is analogous to the previous example, but the term zero (i.e. 0) should be replaced by *item*.

```
public int countItems(int item)
{
   if (list == null)
     return 0;
   else if (firstNodeData() == item)
     return 1 + sublist().countItems(item);
   else
     return sublist().countItems(item);
}
```

5-6) Write a method to return `true` when a linked list has a node containing *item*, and return `false` otherwise.

ALGORITHM 1:

When the list is empty, return `false`; otherwise, if the value of *item* is in the first node, return `true`; if the value of *item* is not in the first node, return the same truth value as the subproblem that checks whether the value of *item* is in the sublist starting from a successor node.

IMPLEMENTATION 1:

```
public boolean itemInList(int item)
{
   if (list == null)
     return false;
   else if (firstNodeData() == item)
     return true;
   else
     return sublist().itemInList(item);
}
```

ALGORITHM 2:

Here is a similar approach for this same problem: If the list is empty, there is no data in it since there are no nodes; otherwise, if the value of *item* is in the list, then it is either in the first node or in the sublist that starts from the second node.

IMPLEMENTATION 2:

```
public boolean itemInList2(int item)
{
   if (list == null)
     return false;
   else
     return (firstNodeData() == item) ||
            sublist().itemInList2(item);
}
```

 7) Let us assume that given linked list can have several nodes with the same data value. Write a method to return a reference to the first node having data equal to *item*. If no node has data equal to *item*, the method should return *null*.

ALGORITHM:

If the list is empty, return *null*; otherwise, if the first node has the value of *item* in it, return a reference to that node. Otherwise, return the same as the method called for the subproblem (for the sublist starting from the successor of the first node).

```
public Node pointToItem(int item)
{
  if (list == null)
     return null;
  else if (firstNodeData() == item)
     return list;
  else
     return sublist().pointToItem(item);
}
```

 8) Write a method to return the reference to the last node that has the value of *item* in the data variable. This assumes that the linked list can have several nodes with the same value in the data variable. If no node has the value of *item* in the data variable, the method should return *null*.

ALGORITHM:

If the list is empty, return *null*; otherwise, let *p* be the result of a recursive call for the subproblem (reference to the last node having *item* in the sublist starting at the successor of the first node). If *p* is *null* and the value of *item* is in the first node, return *list*. If *p* is *null* and the first node does not have the value of *item* in it, return *null*; otherwise, return *p*.

```
public Node pointToLastItem(int item)
{
  Node p;

  if (list == null)
    return null;
  else
  {
     p = sublist().pointToLastItem(item);
     if (p != null)
        return p;
     else
     {
        if (firstNodeData() == item)
          return list;
        else
          return null;
     }
  }
}
```

9) Write a method to return a reference to the *n*-th node in the linked list. It is assumed that the linked list has *n* or more nodes.

ALGORITHM:

If the number *n* is 0, it should return *null*; if the number *n* is 1, the method should return the value *first*, a reference to the first node; otherwise, the method should return the reference that is the result when the same method is called recursively for the sublist starting from the successor node with the number *n*-1.

```
// PRECONDITION: List is nonempty
// Method returns n-th node. When list has fewer than n nodes, method returns null.
public Node return_nth(int n)
{
  if ((n == 0) ||(list == null) || countNodes()<n)
    return null;
  else if (n == 1)
    return list;
  else
    return sublist().return_nth(n-1);
}
```

 10) Write a method to return the sum of the data values of all nodes in the linked list.

ALGORITHM:

If the list is empty, return 0; otherwise, add the value of the data variable of the first node to the sum of the data for the sublist starting from the second node.

```
public int sumData( )
{
  if (list == null)
    return 0;
  else
    return  firstNodeData() + sublist().sumData();
}
```

 11) Write a method to return the product of the data variables of all the nodes in the nonempty linked list. If list is empty return 1.

ALGORITHM:

If the list is empty, return 1; otherwise, multiply the value of the data variable of the first node with the resulting product of the data variable values of the sublist starting from the second node.

```
// For a nonempty list, returns the product of values; and for empty list, returns 1.
 public long product( )
 {
   if (list == null)
     return 1;
   else
     return firstNodeData() * sublist().product();
 }
```

 12) Write a method to return the smallest data value in the nonempty linked list.

ALGORITHM:

If the list has a single node, the method should return the value of the data variable of this node; otherwise, it should return the smaller of the following two values: 1) the data variable of the first node; 2) the smallest value in the sublist starting from the second node.

```
//PRECONDITION: list is nonempty
public int minimum()
{
    int temp;
    if (list.getNext() == null)
       return firstNodeData();
    else
    {
       temp = sublist().minimum();
       if (temp < firstNodeData())
          return temp;
       else
          return firstNodeData();
    }
}
```

 13) Write a method to return a reference to the node with the smallest value in the data variable of the nonempty linked list. Assume that the data in each node have unique values.

ALGORITHM:

If a list has a single node, return a reference to that node; otherwise, the method should return a reference to the node with the smallest data value, which, in this instance, is either the first node, or the node with the smallest data value in the sublist starting from the second node.

```
// PRECONDITION: List is not empty.
// Method returns reference to the node with the smallest data value.
public Node referenceToMin( )
{
  Node  temptr;
  if (list.getNext() == null)
     return list;
  else
  {
     temptr = sublist().referenceToMin();
     if (temptr.getData() < firstNodeData())
       return temptr;
     else
       return list;
  }
}
```

 14) Write a method to return a reference to the node with the smallest data value in the nonempty linked list. When more than one node has the smallest value, return the reference to the last such node.

ALGORITHM:

Similar to example 13 above.

```
// PRECONDITION: List is not empty and data in the nodes is not necessarily unique.
public Node referenceToMin2( )
{
   Node temptr;
   if (list.getNext() == null)
      return list;
   else
   {
      temptr = sublist().referenceToMin2();
      if (temptr.getData() <= firstNodeData())
         return temptr;
```

```
        else
            return list;
    }
}
```

15) Write a method to return the average of the data values in the linked list.

ALGORITHM:

If the list is empty, return 0; if the list has a single node, return the data value of that node; otherwise, let *n* denote the number of nodes in the list. To obtain the average, multiply the average of the sublist (starting from the second node) by *n*-1 and add the value of the first node. Finally, divide the result by *n*.

```
public double average()
{
   if (list == null)
     return 0;
   else if (list.getNext() == null)
     return list.getData();
   else
   {
      int n = countNodes();
      return ((n-1) * sublist().average() + list.getData()) / n;
   }
}
```

16) Write a method to return `true` when the data values of consecutive nodes are sorted in ascending order. If they are not sorted, return `false`.

ALGORITHM:

When the list is empty or when it is a single node list, return `true`; otherwise, if the first node has a value greater than the second node, then return `false`; in all other cases, return the truth value of the subproblem (or, in other words, whether the sublist starting from second node is in ascending order).

```
public boolean isAscending()
{
```

```
  if (list == null)
    return true;
  else if (list.getNext() == null)
    return true;
  else if (list.getData() > sublist().firstNodeData())
    return false;
  else
    return sublist().isAscending();
}
```

 17-18) Write a method to check if the data in this linked list (the one defined in the current class) and the data in the linked list passed as a parameter, *f*, are equal.

ALGORITHM1:

If both lists are empty, return `true`; if both are nonempty, and if both their first nodes have the same data values, then return the same as the subproblem that checks the equality of the sublists starting from the successors of the first nodes; in all other cases, return `false`.

```
public boolean equal(LinkedList f)
{
  if (f.isEmpty() && isEmpty())
    return true;
  else if (!f.isEmpty() && !isEmpty())
  {
    if (f.firstNodeData() == list.getData())
      return sublist().equal(f.sublist());
    else
      return false;
  }
  else
    return false;
}
```

ALGORITHM2:

If a short circuit evaluation is assumed (which is the case in Java), the code is even simpler. If both lists are empty, return `true`; if both lists are nonempty, and their first nodes have the same data values, return the same as the subproblem that checks the equality of their sublists starting from the successors of the first nodes; in all other cases, return `false`.

```
// This different approach can be used when a short circuit evaluation
// of boolean expressions is assumed. The code is simpler in that case.

public boolean equal2(LinkedList f)
{
    if (f.isEmpty() && isEmpty())
      return true;
    else if (!isEmpty() && !f.isEmpty() &&
              f.firstNodeData() == list.getData())
      return sublist().equal2(f.sublist());
    else
      return false;
}
```

19) Increment by one the data value of each node in the linked list.

ALGORITHM:

If the list is nonempty, increment the value of the first node. Next, apply the same procedure to the sublist starting from the successor of the first node.

```
public void addOne()
{
    if (list != null)
    {
        list.setData(list.getData()+1);
        sublist().addOne();
    }
}
```

20) Insert a node with a data value *item* into a sorted linked list. Assume that the data variables of the nodes are arranged in ascending order.

ALGORITHM:

Create a new node with the data value, *item*. If the list is empty, add this newly created node to the list by setting *list* equal to the node. If the list is not empty, and if the value of *item* is less than or equal to the value of the data in the first node of the list, set the *next* field of the newly created node to the value of *list*; next, make the list point to this new node by setting *list* equal to the node. Otherwise, apply the same procedure for the sublist.

```
public void insert(int item)
{
    Node node = new Node (item, null);
    if (list == null)
      list = node;
    else if (firstNodeData() >= item)
    {
      node.setNext(list);
      list = node;
    }
    else
    {
      LinkedList ll = sublist();
      ll.insert(item);
      list.setNext(ll.getFirst());
    }
}
```

 21) Write a method that accepts an array of actual size *n* and creates a linked list whose data variables within the nodes have the values of the array elements in reverse order.

ALGORITHM:

If the size of the array is 0, return a value of *null*; if *n* == 1, create a new node with *data* and *next* variables that have values of *x[0]* and *null,* respectively. Return the linked list with the newly created node. Otherwise, create a linked list with the data from the subarray of the first *n*-1 elements. Create a new node with its *data* equal to the last array element and its *next* referring to the created linked list. Return the linked list with that node.

```
// Input array may be empty or not.
public LinkedList makeLinkedList(int[] x, int n)
{
   if (n == 0)
     return null;
   else if (n == 1)
   {
     Node node = new Node (x[0], null);
     return new LinkedList(node);
   }
   else
   {
     LinkedList ll = makeLinkedList(x, n-1);
```

```
        Node node = new Node (x[n-1], ll.getFirst());
        return new LinkedList(node);
    }
}
```

22) Write a recursive constructor that accepts *firstData*, *n*, and increment *inc* as parameters and initializes the instance variable *list* to refer to the linked list whose data variables have the values equal to: *firstData*, *firstData+inc*, *firstData+2*inc*,. . . , *firstData* + (*n* -1)*inc, respectively.

ALGORITHM:

If the size of the array is 0, let the instance variable *list* have a value of *null*. Otherwise, create a linked list recursively by using *firstData* + *inc*, *n*-1, and *inc*. Create a new node with *firstData* and have its *next* refer to the created linked list. Let the instance variable *list* refer to that node.

```
public LinkedList(int firstData, int n, int inc)
{
   if (n == 0)
      list = null;
   else
   {
      LinkedList ll = new LinkedList(firstData+inc, n-1, inc);
      list = new Node (firstData, ll.getFirst());
   }
}
```

23) Write a recursive constructor that accepts an integer array *arr* and its size, *n*, and initializes the instance variable *list* to refer to the linked list whose data values equal the array elements in reverse order.

ALGORITHM:

If *n* is zero, the list is assigned a value of *null*. Otherwise, invoke the constructor recursively by passing the subarray of *n*-1 elements. Let the instance variable *list* refer to a new node having the data of the last element in the array *x*, and *next* referring to that linked sublist.

```
// Constructor creates linked list of specified size and with node data in reversed order i.e.
// equal to: arr[n-1], arr[n-2],...,arr[1], arr[0].
public LinkedList(int[] arr, int n)
{
```

```
    if (n == 0)
      list = null;
    else
    {
      LinkedList ll = new LinkedList(arr, n-1);
      list = new Node (arr[n-1], ll.getFirst());
    }
}
```

4.2 Private inner class Node storing int data

In section 4.2 the class `Node` is defined as a private class with public variables `data` and `next`. Class `Node` is an inner class within the class `LinkedList`. This arrangement enforces encapsulation for variables `data` and `next`, and provides easy access to these variables. Since `data` and `next` are available within the class `LinkedList`, we do not need methods to get the sublist and data in the first node. In order to provide access to the list and sublist, we only provide public method `getList()` which returns a reference to the beginning of the linked list. All the methods from section 4.1 can be redone by using this design approach. We will only do three of them; the others can be completed by learners as practice.

```java
import java.util.Random;
public class LinkedList
{
    private Node list;

    // Constructor creates linked list of random size and random one digit
    // integer data values. Size must be nonnegative.
    public LinkedList(int size)
    {
      Random r = new Random();
      if (size == 0)
          list = null;
      else if (size == 1)
      {
          Node curr = new Node(Math.abs(r.nextInt()) % 10);
          list=curr;
      }
      else
      {
          LinkedList ll = new LinkedList(size-1);
          Node llList = ll.getList();
          Node curr = new Node(Math.abs(r.nextInt()) % 10);
```

```
            curr.next = llList;
            list = curr;
        }
    }

    //returns the reference to the beginning of the list
    public Node getList()
    {
        return list;
    }

    // prints recursively the data in each node of the linked list
    public void printListRecursively(Node first)
    {
        if (first != null)
        {
            System.out.print(first.data + " ");
            printListRecursively(first.next);
        }
    }

////////////////////////////////////////////////////////////////////////////////////
//  insert recursive methods specified in exercises 24-26 here
////////////////////////////////////////////////////////////////////////////////////

    private class Node
    {
        public int data;
        public Node next;

        public Node()
        {
            next = null;
            data = 0;
        }

        public Node(int data)
        {
            this.data = data;
            next = null;
        }

        public Node (int data, Node next)
        {
            this.data = data;
            this.next = next;
```

```
        }
    } // end class Node
}// end class LinkedList
```

```
public class TestLinkedListRec
{
    public static void main(String[] args)
    {
        LinkedList myList = new LinkedList(3);
        System.out.print("Linked list with 3 random integers");
        myList.printListRec(myList.getList());
        System.out.print("Number of nodes in the linked list: " +
                            myList.countNodes());
        System.out.print("Number of zero nodes in the linked " +
                        "list: " + myList.countZeroNodes());
        System.out.print(" List is sorted: " +
                        myList.isSorted());
    }
}
```

SECTION 4.2 EXAMPLES

 24) Write a method to return the number of nodes in a linked list referred to by the reference *list*.

ALGORITHM:

If the list has no nodes (i.e. it is empty), the method should return 0; otherwise, a nonempty list has one more node than the sublist that starts from the successor of the first node.

```
public int countNodes(Node list)
{
    if (list == null)
        return 0;
    else
        return 1 + countNodes(list.next);
}
```

25) Write a method to return the number of nodes that have a data value equal to zero in a linked list referred to by the reference *list*.

ALGORITHM:

If the list has no nodes (i.e. it is empty), the method should return 0. If the first node has a data value equal to zero, the entire list has one more zero node than the sublist that starts from the successor of the first node; otherwise, the entire list has the same number of zero nodes as the sublist that starts from the successor of the first node.

```
public int countZeroNodes(Node list)
{
   if (list == null)
     return 0;
   else if (list.data == 0)
     return 1 + countZeroNodes(list.next);
   else
     return countZeroNodes(list.next);
}
```

 26) Write a method to return `true` if the data in the list is sorted in ascending order, and `false` otherwise.

ALGORITHM:

If the list has no nodes, or has only one node (i.e. it is empty, or a single node linked list), the method should return `true`. If the first node has a data value that is larger than the data value in the second node, return `false`; otherwise, return the answer for the subproblem.

```
//Return true if the nodes have data in ascending order and false otherwise
public boolean isSorted(Node list)
{
   if (list == null)
     return true;
   else if (list.next == null)
     return true;
   else if (list.data > list.next.data)
     return false;
   else
     return isSorted( list.next );
}
```

4.3 Private inner class StudentNode storing data of Student type

In section 4.3 the variable `data` is an object of `Student` type, defined in a separate independent `Student` class. Since the data are objects, we have to specify how they compare with each other. The method `compareTo` in the `Student` class compares students based on their id. Obviously, this is only one of the many possible ways to compare students. In addition, `data` can be any other type of object as well. Examples 26 through 28 are defined for the classes `StudentNode` and `LinkedListStudent` as specified below. The class `TestLinkedListStudent` contains the main method and is used to test the recursive methods.

```java
public class Student
{
    private String name;
    private String id;
    private int age;
    private double gpa;

    public Student(String n, String i, int a, double g)
    {
        name=n;
        id=i;
        age=a;
        gpa=g;
    }


    // This student is smaller (or equal to or larger ) than student s if it's id is smaller
    // (or equal to or larger than) id for student s
    public int compareTo(Student s)
    {
        return this.id.compareTo( s.id);
    }

    public String toString()
    {
        return name + "\t" + age + "\t" + id + "\t" + gpa;
    }

    public boolean isHonors()
    {
        return (gpa > 3.5);
    }
}
```

```java
public class LinkedListStudent
{
    private StudentNode list;

    public void addFront( Student s)
    {
        StudentNode node = new StudentNode(s);
        node.next = list;
        list = node;
    }

    //returns the reference to the beginning of the list
    public StudentNode getList()
    {
        return list;
    }

//////////////////////////////////////////////////////////////////////////////
//
//   insert recursive methods specified in the exercises 27) – 30) here
//
//////////////////////////////////////////////////////////////////////////////

    private class StudentNode
    {
      public Student data;
      public StudentNode next;

      public StudentNode (Student data)
      {
        this.data = data;
        next = null;
      }

      public StudentNode (Student data, StudentNode next)
      {
        this.data = data;
        this.next = next;
      }
    } // end class StudentNode

} // end class LinkedListStudent
```

```
public class TestLinkedListStudent
{
  public static void main(String[] args)
  {
    LinkedListStudent ll = new LinkedListStudent();
    ll.addFront(new Student("John", "107", 33, 3.7));
    ll.addFront(new Student("John", "105", 20, 3.7));
    ll.addFront(new Student("Anna", "102", 22, 2.9));
    ll.printListRecursive(ll.getList());

    System.out.println("Number of nodes: " +
                          ll.countNodes(ll.getList()));

///////////////////////////////////////////////////////////////////////////////
// Write code to test the recursive methods  for examples 28) – 30)
///////////////////////////////////////////////////////////////////////////////
  }
}
```

SECTION 4.3 EXAMPLES

27) Write a method to return the number of nodes in a linked list referred to by the reference *list*.

ALGORITHM:

If the list has no nodes (i.e. it is empty), the method should return 0; otherwise, a nonempty list has one more node than the sublist that starts from the successor of the first node.

```
public int countNodes(StudentNode list)
{
  if (list == null)
    return 0;
  else
    return 1 + countNodes(list.next);
}
```

28) Write a method to return the number of honors students in the given linked list referred to by the reference *list*.

ALGORITHM:

If the list is empty return zero. Otherwise, check if the student in the first node is an honors student. If it is, return 1 plus the number of honors students in the sublist, otherwise return the number of honors students in the sublist.

```java
// Returns number of honors students in the list
public int countHonors(StudentNode list)
{
    if(list == null)
        return 0;
    else if (list.data.isHonors())
        return 1 + countHonors(list.next);
    else
        return countHonors(list.next);
}
```

29) Write a method to print the data for each student in a linked list referred to by the reference *list*.

ALGORITHM:

If the list is empty do nothing; otherwise, print the data for the first node and call the recursive subproblem to print each student in a sublist that starts from the successor of the first node.

```java
public void printListRecursive(StudentNode list)
{
    if (list != null)
    {
        System.out.print(list.data + "\n");
        printListRecursive(list.next);
    }
}
```

30) Write a method to return `true` if the list has its nodes sorted in ascending order by the Student type data, return `false` otherwise. NOTE: there are three base cases: empty list, single node list, and list where the first two nodes have students that are out of order.
ALGORITHM:

If the list is empty or has only one node, the method should return `true`; if the first node has data that is larger than the data in the second node, return `false`; otherwise return the answer for the subproblem.

```
// Return true if nodes have data in ascending order and false otherwise
public boolean isSorted (StudentNode list)
{
    if (list== null)
       return true;
    else if (list.next == null)
       return true;
    else if (list.data.compareTo(list.next.data)>0)
       return false;
    else
       return isSorted( list.next );
}
```

CHAPTER 5   EXAMPLES ON LINKED TREES

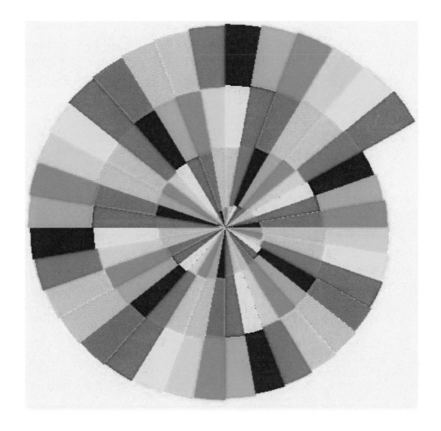

Recursive methods dealing with linked trees

Examples include: count tree nodes, return reference to node with smallest data, traverse
list inorder, preorder, postorder, count tree leaves, count internal nodes, make tree that is
mirror image, and similar.

In the examples that follow, we will write recursive methods for a given binary tree. Reference `root` refers to the root node of a linked binary tree. The base case is usually when the tree is empty, or when it has only one node, or sometimes both. The recursive step specifies how to solve the problem on a given tree by using the solutions gained from performing simpler tasks specified for the left and right subtrees.

Class `TreeNode` describes nodes in the tree. Nodes in the class `TreeNode` store data of integer type for simplicity. A more general approach would require using variant type.

The class `LinkedTree` has a private instance variable `root`, and private auxiliary methods `isEmpty()`, `rootValue()`, `leftSubtree()`, and `rightSubtree()`. The method names are self-descriptive and they indicate the method's functionality. All the recursive methods that will be discussed are part of the class `LinkedTree`. If the recursive methods were part of any descendant class of the class `LinkedTree`, the auxiliary methods would have to have protected visibility instead of being private. The constructor creates the following tree as the default:

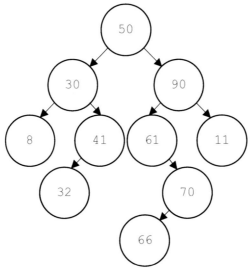

Figure 5   Default example of a tree

One can also implement a different constructor to create a random tree of a different specified size or shape, or a tree of random size and shape. Those additional constructors could be implemented as recursive methods as additional practice examples.

One such constructor that creates a random tree with specified n nodes where n is a positive integer is provided in example 29.

Analogous to the linked list approach, we can implement a linked tree with a private class for `TreeNode` and public data in it. In addition, the data type for the `TreeNode` data may be any kind of object. We leave the above implementation as an exercise.

```java
public class TreeNode
{
  private int data;
  private TreeNode left;
  private TreeNode right;

  public TreeNode()                  // Creates node with no data assigned yet
  {
    left = null;
    right = null;
  }

  public TreeNode(int item)     // Creates new node with item stored as data
  {
    data = item;
    left = null;
    right = null;
  }

  public String toString()        // Returns String representation of data
  {
    return Integer.toString(data);
  }

  public TreeNode getLeft()
  {
    return left;
  }

  public TreeNode getRight()
  {
    return right;
  }
```

```
  public int getData()
  {
    return data;
  }

  public void setLeft(TreeNode l)
  {
    left = l;
  }

  public void setRight(TreeNode r)
  {
    right = r;
  }

  public void setData( int d)
  {
    data = d;
  }
}
```

```
public class LinkedTree
{
  private TreeNode root;

  public LinkedTree()        // Creates default linked tree shown above
  {
    root = new TreeNode(50);
    root.setLeft(new TreeNode(30));
    root.setRight(new TreeNode(90));
    TreeNode l = root.getLeft();
    l.setLeft(new TreeNode(8));
    l.setRight(new TreeNode(41));
    TreeNode lr = l.getRight();
    root.getLeft().getRight();
    lr.setLeft(new TreeNode(32));
    TreeNode r = root.getRight();
    r.setLeft(new TreeNode(61));
    r.setRight(new TreeNode(11));
    TreeNode rl = r.getLeft();
    rl.setRight(new TreeNode(70));
    TreeNode rlr = rl.getRight();
    rlr.setLeft(new TreeNode(66));
  }
```

```
    public LinkedTree(TreeNode r)          // Creates linked tree with root r
    {
      root = r;
    }

    private int rootValue()                // Returns data stored in the root node
    {
      return root.getData();
    }

    private TreeNode getRoot()             // Returns reference to the root of the tree
    {
      return root;
    }

    private LinkedTree leftSubtree()    // Returns left subtree
    {
      return new LinkedTree(root.getLeft());
    }

    private LinkedTree rightSubtree()// Returns right subtree
    {
      return new LinkedTree(root.getRight());
    }

    private boolean isEmpty()       // Returns true if tree is empty and false if it is not
    {
      return root==null;
    }

/////////////////////////////////////////////////////////////////////////////////////////////////////
// All the recursive methods in the examples listed in this chapter should be inserted here
/////////////////////////////////////////////////////////////////////////////////////////////////////

}  // end class LinkedTree
```

EXAMPLES

1) Write a method to return the number of nodes in a linked binary tree.

ALGORITHM:

If the tree referred to by *root* is an empty tree, the method should return 0. Otherwise, the number of nodes in the whole tree (referred to by *root*) is the sum of:

- the number of nodes in the left subtree,
- the number of nodes in the right subtree, and
- 1 (add 1 for the root node).

```
public int countNodes()
{
  if (isEmpty())
    return 0;
  else
    return 1+leftSubtree().countNodes() +
            rightSubtree().countNodes();
}
```

 2) For a given linked binary tree, write a method to return the number of nodes with data value equal to zero.

ALGORITHM:

For the clarity of the text, we will refer to the nodes having value zero in the data variable as the zeronodes. If the tree is empty, there are no nodes at all and consequently the number of zeronodes is also 0. Otherwise, if the node referred to by *root* has data equal to zero, then the number of zeronodes in the whole tree is 1 more than the number of zeronodes in the left subtree plus the number of zeronodes in the right subtree. Finally, the number of zeronodes in a nonempty tree whose root node does not have value zero is equal to the number of zeronodes in the left subtree plus the number of zeronodes in the right subtree.

```
public int countZeroNodes()
{
  if (isEmpty())
    return 0;
  else if (rootValue() == 0)
    return leftSubtree().countZeroNodes()+
            rightSubtree().countZeroNodes() + 1;
  else
    return leftSubtree().countZeroNodes() +
            rightSubtree().countZeroNodes();
}
```

3) Count the number of leaves in a linked binary tree. A leaf is a node with no children.

ALGORITHM:

If a tree is empty it has no leaves, and, consequently, the total number of leaves is zero. Otherwise, if the tree has only one node, the total number of leaves is one since this is the only leaf in the tree. Finally, the total number of leaves in the tree is the sum of the total number of leaves in the left and right subtrees.

```
public int countLeaves()
{
  if (isEmpty())
    return 0;
  else if ( root.getLeft() == null &&
           root.getRight() == null )
    return 1;
  else
    return leftSubtree().countLeaves() +
           rightSubtree().countLeaves();
}
```

4) Count the number of non-leaf nodes in a given linked binary tree. A non-leaf node has at least one child.

ALGORITHM:

If the tree is empty, it has no nodes (and no non-leaves as well), and, consequently, the total number of non-leaf nodes is zero. If the tree has a single node, then this node is a leaf, and the number of non-leaf nodes is 0. All other types of trees have 1 more non-leaf node than the sum of non-leaf nodes in both subtrees.

```
public int countNonLeaves()
{
  if ( isEmpty() )
    return 0;
  else if ( root.getLeft() == null &&
           root.getRight() == null )
    return 0;
  else
    return leftSubtree().countNonLeaves() +
           rightSubtree().countNonLeaves() + 1;
}
```

5) For a given binary tree, return the reference to the node having the data value *item*. If no node in the tree has *item* as its data value, the method should return *null*. It is assumed that each node's data has a unique value.

ALGORITHM:

If the tree is empty, it has no nodes, and, consequently, there are no nodes whose data is equal to *item*. So, the method returns *null*. Otherwise, if the root node's data is equal to *item*, a reference *root* is returned. If it is not equal to *item*, the presence of a node whose data is equal to *item* is checked for in the left subtree. If found, a reference to that node is returned. If no node has data equal to *item*, then the answer for the presence of a node with data equal to *item* in the right subtree is returned.

```
public TreeNode pointToItem(int item)
{
  TreeNode temp = null;
  if (isEmpty())
    return null;
  else if (rootValue() == item)
    return root;
  else
  {
    temp = leftSubtree().pointToItem(item);
    if (temp != null)
      return temp;
    else
      return rightSubtree().pointToItem(item);
  }
}
```

6) Write a method to return the sum of data values in all nodes in the given linked binary tree.

ALGORITHM:

If the tree referred to by *root* is an empty tree, the method should return 0. Otherwise, the sum of the data values in all nodes in the linked tree is the sum of:

- the sum of the data values in all the nodes in the left subtree,
- the sum of the data values in all the nodes in the right subtree and
- the value of the data in the root node.

```
public int sumData( )
{
  if (isEmpty())
    return 0;
  else
    return leftSubtree().sumData() + rootValue() +
            rightSubtree().sumData();
}
```

 7) Return the product of all data values in the given linked binary tree, returning 1 when the tree is empty.

ALGORITHM:

If the tree is empty, 1 is returned, as per the problem description. Otherwise, in the case of a nonempty tree, the product of the data values of all the nodes in the tree is the product of:

- the product of the data values of all the nodes in the left subtree,
- the product of the data values of all the nodes in the right subtree and
- the value of the data variable in the root node.

```
public int product()
{
  if (isEmpty())
    return 1;
  else
    return leftSubtree().product() * rightSubtree().product() *
            rootValue();
}
```

 8) Perform an inorder traversal of the linked tree.

ALGORITHM:

If the tree is empty, there is nothing to be done. Otherwise, perform an inorder traversal of the left subtree, display the root node value, and then perform an inorder traversal of the right subtree.

```
public void traverseInOrder()
{
  if (!isEmpty())
```

```
    {
      leftSubtree().traverseInOrder();
      System.out.println(rootValue());
      rightSubtree().traverseInOrder();
    }
}
```

 9) Perform a preorder traversal of the given linked binary tree.

ALGORITHM:

If the tree is empty, there is nothing to be done. Otherwise, display the root node value, perform a preorder traversal of the left subtree, and then perform preorder traversal of the right subtree.

```
public void traversePreOrder()
{
  if (!isEmpty())
    {
      System.out.println(rootValue());
      leftSubtree().traversePreOrder();
      rightSubtree().traversePreOrder();
    }
}
```

 10) Perform a postorder traversal of the linked binary tree.

ALGORITHM:

If the tree is empty, there is nothing to be done. Otherwise, perform a postorder traversal of the left subtree, perform a postorder traversal of the right subtree, and then display the root node value.

```
public void traversePostOrder()
{
  if (!isEmpty())
    {
      leftSubtree().traversePostOrder();
      rightSubtree().traversePostOrder();
      System.out.println(rootValue());
    }
}
```

11) For a given linked binary tree, increment the data value of each node in the tree by one.

ALGORITHM:

If the tree is empty, there is nothing to do. Otherwise, increment the data variable value of the root node, increment all the values in the left subtree, and then increment all the values in the right subtree.

```
Public void incrementByOne()
{
  if (!isEmpty())
  {
    root.setData(rootValue() +1);
    leftSubtree().incrementByOne();
    rightSubtree().incrementByOne();
  }
}
```

 12) Return the smallest data value in the given linked binary tree. When the tree is empty, the method returns the *largest integer*. (NOTE: Java Integer wrapper class contains a static constant Integer.MAX_VALUE).

ALGORITHM:

If the tree is empty, Integer.MAX_VALUE is returned as per the problem description. Otherwise, in the case of a nonempty tree, the smallest data value of all the nodes in the linked tree (referred to by *root*) is the smallest of:
- the smallest data value of all the nodes in the left subtree,
- the smallest data value of all the nodes in the right subtree and
- the value of the data variable in the root node.

```
//PRECONDITION: data values stored in the tree nodes are integers
public int minimum()
{
  if (isEmpty())
    return Integer.MAX_VALUE;
  else
    return Math.min(rootValue(),
                  Math.min(leftSubtree().minimum(),
                          rightSubtree().minimum()));
}
```

13-14) Method returns the reference to the node with the smallest data value in a given linked binary tree. If the tree is empty, it returns *null*.

ALGORITHM 1:

If the tree is empty, *null* is returned as per the problem description. Otherwise, in the case of a nonempty tree, assume the root node holds the smallest data value of all the nodes in the linked tree. Next, find the reference to the node with the smallest value in the left subtree. If this is not null and its data value is smaller than the data in the root node, we change our assumption. Subsequently, we find the reference to the node with the smallest value in the right subtree and perform the same check again. Finally, we return the assumption as our final answer.

IMPLEMENTATION 1:

```
public TreeNode referenceToMinimum()
{
  TreeNode ans, temp;
  if (isEmpty())
    return null;
  else
  {
    ans = root;
    temp = leftSubtree().referenceToMinimum();
    if (temp != null && temp.getData() < ans.getData())
      ans = temp;
    temp = rightSubtree().referenceToMinimum();
    if (temp != null && temp.getData() < ans.getData())
      ans = temp;
    return ans;
  }
}
```

ALGORITHM 2:

If the tree is empty, *null* is returned. If the tree has a single node, *root* is returned. Otherwise, if the left subtree is empty, the recursive subproblem is called to return the reference *r* that refers to the node with the smallest data in the right subtree. After comparing the data at *root* and at *r*, the reference referring to the node with smaller data is returned. If the left subtree is not empty but the right subtree is, the recursive subproblem is called to return the reference *l* that refers to the node with the smallest data in the left subtree. After comparing the data at *root* and at *l*, the reference referring to the node with smaller data is returned. If both left and right subtrees are nonempty, call two recursive subproblems to get references *l* and *r* that refer to the node with smallest data in the left and right subtrees, respectively. Compare data at *l*, at *r*, and at *root*, and return the reference that refers to the node with the smallest data of those three.

IMPLEMENTATION 2:

```
public TreeNode referenceToMinimum()
{
  TreeNode l, r, min;
  if (isEmpty())
    return null;
  else if ( root.getLeft() == null && root.getRight()== null )
    return root;
  else if (root.getLeft() == null)
  {
    r = rightSubtree().referenceToMinimum();
    if (r.getData() < rootValue())
      return r;
    else
      return root;
  }
  else if (root.getRight() == null)
  {
    l = leftSubtree().referenceToMinimum();
    if (l.getData() < rootValue())
      return l;
    else
      return root;
  }
  else
  {
    l = leftSubtree().referenceToMinimum();
    r = rightSubtree().referenceToMinimum();
    min = l;
    if (r.getData() < min.getData())
      min = r;
    if (rootValue() < min.getData())
      min = root;
    return min;
  }
}
```

 15) Return the depth of the given linked binary tree. The depth of an empty tree is -1. The depth for a general tree is the longest distance from the root to a leaf node.

ALGORITHM:

If the tree is empty, -1 is returned. Otherwise, the depth is one more than the depth of the deeper of the two subtrees.

```
public int depth()
{
  if (isEmpty())
    return -1;
  else
    return 1 + Math.max(leftSubtree().depth(),
                         rightSubtree().depth());
}
```

 16) Determine the depth of a given *item* in the linked binary tree. The method should return the distance from the root node to the node containing *item*. Assume that each node has a unique data. Return -1 for either an empty tree or a tree that does not contain the *item*.

ALGORITHM:

If the tree is empty, -1 is returned as per problem description. If *item* is in the root node, 0 is returned as the answer. Otherwise, the left subtree is checked for the depth of *item*, and, if found, 1 more than the distance of the node containing *item* from the root of the left subtree is returned. The same check is performed on the right subtree next. A similar result is returned if found. Finally, if it was not found, -1 is returned.

```
public int itemDepth(int item)
{
  int depthLeft, depthRight;
  if (isEmpty())
    return -1;
  else if (rootValue() == item)
    return 0;
  else            // nonempty tree whose root node does not contain item
  {
    depthLeft = leftSubtree().itemDepth(item);
    if (depthLeft != -1)
      return 1 + depthLeft;
    depthRight = rightSubtree().itemDepth(item);
    if (depthRight != -1)
      return 1 + depthRight;
    else
```

```
      return -1;
   }
}
```

 17) Measure the depth of a given *item* in the linked binary tree. If more than one node has the value *item,* return the distance from the root node to the closest node containing *item*. Return -1 for an empty tree or a tree that does not contain the *item.*

ALGORITHM:

If the tree is empty, return -1. Otherwise, if *item* is in the root node, return 0. For a nonempty tree whose root node does not contain *item*, if neither subtree is empty and have *item*, return 1 plus the distance to the node containing *item* of the shorter subtree. Otherwise, if only the left subtree is not empty and contains *item*, return 1 plus the distance to the node containing *item* of the left subtree. Similarly, if only the right subtree is not empty and contains *item*, return 1 plus the distance to the node containing *item* of the right subtree. Finally, in the case that the tree does not contain *item*, return -1.

```java
public int closestItemDepth(int item)
{
   int depthLeft, depthRight;
   if (isEmpty())
      return -1;
   else if (rootValue() == item)
      return 0;
   else
   {
      depthLeft = leftSubtree().closestItemDepth(item);
      depthRight = rightSubtree().closestItemDepth(item);
      if (depthRight != -1 && depthLeft != -1)
         return 1 + Math.min(depthLeft, depthRight);
      else if (depthLeft != -1)
         return 1 + depthLeft;
      else if (depthRight != -1)
         return 1 + depthRight;
      else
         return -1;
   }
}
```

18) For a given linked binary tree return `true` if at least one of the nodes contains *item* in the data variable and return `false` otherwise.

ALGORITHM:

If the tree is empty return `false`. If there are no nodes in the tree, there can be no nodes containing item either. If the root node contains *item*, return `true`; otherwise (when the root node does not have *item* in it, item can still be either in the left or in the right subtree), return `true` if *item* is in the left or in the right subtree, and `false` otherwise.

IMPLEMENTATION 1:

```
public boolean itemInTree ( int item)
{
  if (isEmpty())
    return false;
  else if (rootValue() == item)
    return true;
  else
    return leftSubtree().itemInTree(item) ||
           rightSubtree().itemInTree(item);
}
```

Java applies short circuit evaluation by default. This allows us to combine the entire if-else if-else statement into one in the following implementation.

IMPLEMENTATION 2:

```
public boolean itemInTree2(int item)
{
  if (isEmpty())
    return false;
  else
    return (rootValue() == item ||
           leftSubtree().itemInTree2(item) ||
           rightSubtree().itemInTree2(item) );
}
```

19) Check whether or not a given linked binary tree referred to by *root* is a binary search tree (BST). Assume that BST has unique data in every node.

ALGORITHM:

An empty tree and a single node tree can be considered a BST, so return `true`. In the case that the left subtree is empty, if the root data is greater than the data of the right child, return `false`. Otherwise, return the answer for the right subtree. In the case that the right subtree is empty, if the data of the left child is greater than the data of the root, return `false`. Otherwise, return the same answer as for the subproblem of the left subtree. Finally, if both subtrees are nonempty and the root data is both greater than the data of the left child and the root data is less than the data of the right child then return the value of the conjunction of the values for the subproblems for the left and right subtrees. Otherwise, return `false`.

```
public boolean isBST()
{
  if (isEmpty())
    return true;
  else if ( root.getLeft()== null &&
            root.getRight() == null )
    return true;
  else if (root.getLeft() == null)
  {
    if (rootValue()< rightSubtree().rootValue())
      return rightSubtree().isBST();
    else
      return false;
  }
  else if (root.getRight() == null)
  {
    if (leftSubtree().rootValue()< rootValue())
      return leftSubtree().isBST();
    else
      return false;
  }
  else if ( leftSubtree().rootValue() < rootValue() &&
            rootValue() < rightSubtree().rootValue())
    return leftSubtree().isBST() && rightSubtree().isBST();
  else
    return false;
}
```

20) For a given linked binary tree, count the leaf nodes having an odd data value.

ALGORITHM:

If the tree is empty, 0 is returned. If the tree has a single node whose data value is odd, return 1; otherwise, return the sum of the answers for the subproblems defined on the left and the right subtree.

```
public int countOddLeaves()
{
  if (isEmpty())
     return 0;
  else if (root.getLeft() == null && rootValue()%2 == 1
          && root.getRight() == null )
     return 1;
  else
     return leftSubtree().countOddLeaves()+
          rightSubtree().countOddLeaves();
}
```

 21) For a given linked binary tree, count the nonleaf nodes having an even data value.

ALGORITHM:

If the tree is empty or has only one node, 0 is returned. Otherwise, if the data variable of the root is even, return the sum of answers for the two subproblems defined on the left and right subtree plus 1. Finally, if the data variable is odd return the sum of answers for the two subproblems defined on the left and right subtree.

```
public int countEvenNonLeaves()
{
  if (isEmpty() || (root.getLeft() == null &&
                    root.getRight() == null))
     return 0;
  else
  {
    if (rootValue() % 2 == 0)
      return leftSubtree().countEvenNonLeaves() +
             rightSubtree().countEvenNonLeaves() + 1;
    else
```

```
        return leftSubtree().countEvenNonLeaves() +
                rightSubtree().countEvenNonLeaves();
    }
}
```

 22) For a given linked binary tree, count the leaf nodes having a positive data value.

ALGORITHM:

The same as example 16 with the exception that the condition, "data value is odd", should be replaced by "data value is positive".

```
public int countPositiveLeaves()
{
  if (isEmpty())
    return 0;
  else if (rootValue() > 0 && root.getLeft() == null
                         && root.getRight() == null)
    return 1;
  else
    return leftSubtree().countPositiveLeaves()+
           rightSubtree().countPositiveLeaves();
}
```

 23) For a given linked binary tree, count the nonleaf nodes having a negative data value.

ALGORITHM:

The same as example 21 with the exception that the condition, "data is even", should be replaced by "data is negative".

```
public int countNegativeNonLeaves()
{
  if (isEmpty() || (root.getLeft() == null &&
                    root.getRight() == null))
    return 0;
  else if (rootValue() < 0)
    return leftSubtree().countNegativeNonLeaves() +
           rightSubtree().countNegativeNonLeaves() + 1;
```

```
   else
      return leftSubtree().countNegativeNonLeaves() +
             rightSubtree().countNegativeNonLeaves();
}
```

 24) Write a method that transforms the given linked binary tree, into its mirror image.

ALGORITHM:

For a nonempty tree, change the left link from the root node to refer to the right subtree and the right link to refer to the left subtree. Then make a mirror image of the left and a mirror image of the right subtree.

```
public void mirrorTree()
{
   TreeNode t;
   if (!isEmpty())
   {
      t = root.getLeft();
      root.setLeft(root.getRight());
      root.setRight( t );
      leftSubtree().mirrorTree();
      rightSubtree().mirrorTree();
   }
}
```

 25) Make a copy of a given linked binary tree. The method should create new nodes for this new tree and copy the data variables from the old tree to the new one.

ALGORITHM:

When the original tree is empty, a copy of the tree is also an empty tree. Otherwise, create a new node and put the data variable of the root as its data and then apply the same procedure recursively to its left and right subtrees.

```
public LinkedTree copyTree()
{
   TreeNode t = null;
   if (isEmpty())
      return new LinkedTree(null);
   else
```

```
    {
        t = new TreeNode(rootValue());
        t.setRight(rightSubtree().copyTree().getRoot());
        t.setLeft(leftSubtree().copyTree().getRoot());
        return new LinkedTree(t);
    }
}
```

 26) Write a method to print a given linked binary tree by applying inorder traversal.

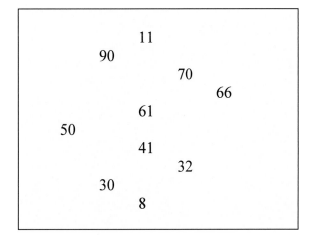

Figure 6   Result of printTree method invocation

ALGORITHM:

Inorder traversal lists the data values of all the nodes, but does not provide the shape of the tree. Our tree will have the root placed in the leftmost position. All nodes that are at the same depth should be vertically aligned. The children of a node are placed five characters to the right of the parent node. In addition, the left child of a node is displayed below it and the right child is displayed above it. This gives the tree a left to right shape as opposed to the usual top down look.

Use the recursive method inorderTraversal as a guide. Modify it by adding int parameter *level* which represents level or depth of a current node. The functionality of the method printTree is similar to inorderTraversal. The difference is that the left and right subtree make recursive calls by incrementing the argument, and are invoked in reverse order. In addition, the data value of the node is displayed shifted by *level* times five characters to the right.

If a tree is created using a default constructor, and printTree method is applied, the outcome should be as shown in Figure 6.

```
public void printTree(int level)
{
  if (!isEmpty())
  {
     rightSubtree().printTree(level + 1);
     for( int i=1; i<level*5; i++)
        System.out.print(" ");
     System.out.println(rootValue());
     leftSubtree().printTree(level + 1);
  }
}
```

 27) Write a method to transform a given binary tree into a complete binary tree of the same depth. The additional nodes' data values should be set to -1 (sentinel value).

ALGORITHM:

Use the recursive method `completeTree` with the int parameter *depth* representing the depth of a given binary tree. When *depth* is zero there is nothing to do. Otherwise, for each nonexistent child create one with the sentinel data value. Afterwards, for each child node, create a linked tree with it as the root and invoke the method recursively with a decremented *depth* on the newly created tree.

```
public void completeTree(int depth)
{
  if ( depth != 0 )
  {
    if (root.getLeft() == null)
      root.setLeft( new TreeNode(-1));
    if (root.getRight() == null)
      root.setRight(new TreeNode(-1));
    new LinkedTree(root.getLeft()).completeTree(depth - 1);
    new LinkedTree(root.getRight()).completeTree(depth- 1);
  }
}
```

 28) Write a method to print a complete linked binary tree in the way it is described in example 26.

All nodes with the data variable having a sentinel value (-1) are considered nonexistent and should be displayed as "--". The rest of the nodes should be displayed by printing the data.

If the tree is a default tree, created by using the `LinkedTree()` constructor, and the method `completeTree(4)` is applied to it, followed by invoking the `printCompleteTree(1)` method, the resulting tree should be as shown in Figure 7.

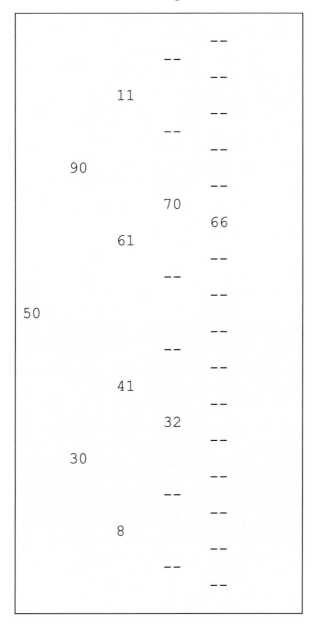

Figure 7   Result of printCompleteTree method invocation

ALGORITHM:

The algorithm is similar to the one used in the example 26. The difference is in the way the nodes are displayed. Method displayNode from TreeNode class is overloaded to display regular nodes by printing their data value, and for nodes with a sentinel value by printing "--".

```
public void printCompleteTree(int level)
{
    if (!isEmpty())
    {
      rightSubtree().printCompleteTree(level + 1);
      for( int i=1; i<level*5; i++)
        System.out.print(" ");
      if (rootValue() == -1)
        System.out.println("—");
      else
        System.out.println(rootValue());
      leftSubtree().printCompleteTree(level + 1);
    }
}
```

 29) Write another constructor in the class LinkedTree to generate a random tree with *n* nodes and data in the range from zero to a predefined constant C.

ALGORITHM:

Use the recursive method createTree with two parameters. The first parameter indicates the number of nodes in the tree, and the second parameter is a reference to the root of the tree. The method returns a reference to the generated tree.

It has two base cases. When parameter *n* equals zero, the tree is empty, and method returns *null*. When *n* equals one, it sets the left and the right variables of the parameter *t* to *null*, and returns *t*. Otherwise, the number *nn*, in the range from zero to *n* minus one, is generated to specify the number of nodes in the left subtree.

The number of nodes in the right subtree is determined so that the total number in both subtrees plus one for the node itself adds up to *n*. The number of nodes in the right subtree is *n* - *nn* - 1. The left and right subtrees are created by appropriate recursive calls.

```
final static int C = 100;

public LinkedTree(int n)
{
    root = createTree(n, new TreeNode((int)(Math.random() * C)));
}
```

```java
private TreeNode createTree(int n, TreeNode t)
{
  if (n == 0)
    return null;
  else if (n == 1)
  {
    t.setLeft( null );
    t.setRight( null );
    return t;
  }
  else
  {
    int nn = (int)(Math.random() * n);

    TreeNode tLeft = new TreeNode((int)(Math.random()*C));
    t.setLeft(createTree(nn, tLeft));

    TreeNode tRight = new TreeNode((int)(Math.random()*C));
    t.setRight(createTree(n-nn-1, tRight));
  }
  return t;
}
```

CHAPTER 6   GRAPHICAL EXAMPLES

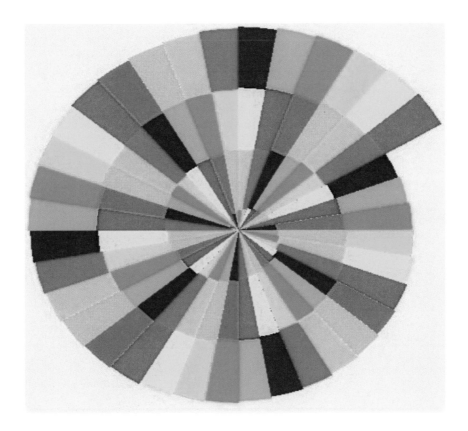

Recursive methods that draw various shapes on graphical surface

Examples include: drawing parallel lines, concentric circles, butterfly squares, c-curve, dragon-curve, Sierpinski triangles, broccoli, spiral, and similar.

In this section we start with simple recursive methods to draw collections of lines, rectangles, or ovals on a graphical surface. At the end of the chapter we draw fractal curves such as C-curve, Dragon-curve, Tree and Broccoli that are more complex. For each example, we provide a complete JavaFX application that defines the required recursive method, and invokes it in the method `start`. We also show the resulting picture.

Recursive steps typically include one or more recursive calls and may draw desired shapes in addition to that. The base case usually includes code to draw some basic drawing. In some cases, in the base case, nothing is done, and it just serves as a stopper for the recursion.

The main advantage of using graphics is that drawing shapes naturally provides a visualization of the steps performed by recursion. After completing several simple practice examples learners typically understand better how to write recursive methods.

EXAMPLES

 1) Design an application with a recursive method to draw vertical parallel lines that are DIST apart from each other and DIST away from all four window borders. Picture shows resulting lines.

Drawing a line typically requires four parameters $x1, y1, x2, y2$ which are the coordinates of the two end points. Vertical parallel lines all have the same value for $y1$ and $y2$ where $y1$=DIST and $y2$ = SIZE-DIST since all lines have to be DIST away from the top and from the bottom of the window. Also $x1 = x2$ for each line since lines are vertical.

The recursive method to draw vertical parallel lines requires only two parameters: x representing the distance of a line from the left border of the window, and *group* that is displayed on the scene. The method will be called by passing DIST for x, since we want the first line to be DIST away from the left border.

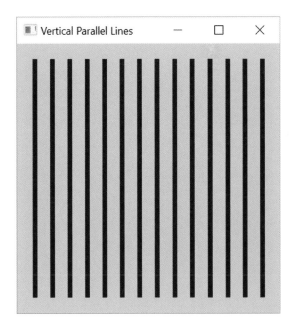

The task of drawing vertical equidistant lines will be completed when *x* is larger than the size of the window minus DIST. If *x* >= SIZE, we do nothing; otherwise, we draw one vertical line that is *x* away from the left border of the window, and, in addition, we call the method recursively with parameter *x* + DIST to draw the remaining lines.

```
import javafx.application.Application;
import javafx.scene.Group;
import javafx.scene.Scene;
import javafx.scene.paint.Color;
import javafx.scene.shape.*;
import javafx.stage.Stage;

public class VerticalLines extends Application
{
    public final int SIZE = 300;
    public final int DIST = 20;

    public void vLines(int x, Group group)
    {
        Line line;
        if (x < SIZE)
        {
            line = new Line(x, DIST, x, SIZE-DIST);
            line.setStrokeWidth(5);
            line.setStroke(Color.NAVY);
            group.getChildren().add( line);
            vLines(x + DIST, group);
```

```
        }
    }

    public void start(Stage stage) throws Exception
    {
        Group group = new Group();
        Scene scene = new Scene(group, SIZE, SIZE, Color.PINK);
        vLines(DIST, group);
        stage.setTitle("Vertical Parallel Lines");
        stage.setScene(scene);
        stage.show();
    }

    public static void main(String[] args)
    {
        launch(args);
    }
}
```

2) Design a JavaFX application with a recursive method to draw horizontal parallel lines that are DIST apart from each other and DIST away from all four borders of the window. Picture shows the resulting lines.

This is similar to previous example except that this time the recursive method uses one parameter *y* to specify the distance of the line from the top and a graphics parameter to draw on.

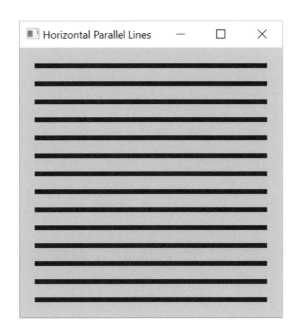

```
import javafx.application.Application;
import javafx.scene.Group;
import javafx.scene.Scene;
import javafx.scene.paint.Color;
import javafx.scene.shape.*;
import javafx.stage.Stage;

public class HorizontalLines extends Application
{
    public final int SIZE = 300;
    public final int DIST = 20;

    public void hLines(int y, Group group)
    {
        Line line;
        if (y < SIZE)
        {
            line = new Line(DIST, y, SIZE-DIST, y);
            line.setStrokeWidth(5);
            line.setStroke(Color.NAVY);
            group.getChildren().add( line);
            hLines(y + DIST, group);
        }
    }

    public void start(Stage stage) throws Exception
    {
        Group group = new Group();
        Scene scene = new Scene(group, SIZE, SIZE, Color.PINK);
        hLines(DIST, group);
        stage.setTitle("Horizontal Parallel Lines");
        stage.setScene(scene);
        stage.show();
    }

    public static void main(String[] args)
    {
        launch(args);
    }
}
```

3) Draw vertical parallel lines that are DIST apart from each other and DIST away from the left, bottom, and right borders of the window. Each next line is DIST shorter than the previous one. All lines have bottom points with same *y* since they are all DIST apart from the bottom edge.

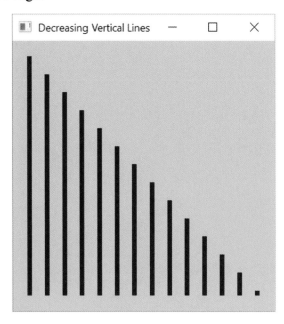

```java
import javafx.application.Application;
import javafx.scene.Group;
import javafx.scene.Scene;
import javafx.scene.paint.Color;
import javafx.scene.shape.*;
import javafx.stage.Stage;

public class DecreasingVerticalLines extends Application
{
    public final int SIZE = 300;
    public final int DIST = 20;

    public void vLines(int x, Group group)
    {
        Line line;
        if (x < SIZE)
        {
            line = new Line(x, x, x, SIZE-DIST);
            line.setStrokeWidth(5);
            line.setStroke(Color.NAVY);
            group.getChildren().add( line);
```

```
            vLines(x + DIST, group);
        }
    }

    public void start(Stage stage) throws Exception
    {
        Group group = new Group();
        Scene scene = new Scene(group, SIZE, SIZE, Color.PINK);
        vLines(DIST, group);
        stage.setTitle(" Decreasing Vertical Lines");
        stage.setScene(scene);
        stage.show();
    }

    public static void main(String[] args)
    {
        launch(args);
    }
}
```

 4) Draw squares so that all of them have the same center. The largest square is DIST apart from the window borders. Window has dimension SIZExSIZE. Each next square is DIST apart from the previous one.

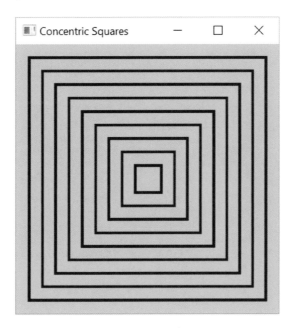

The upper left corner of each square has same value for both *x* and *y*. Let's call it *xy*. Since we draw squares, the width and height have the same value equal to SIZE − 2 * *xy*. Value *xy* is subtracted twice because a square is *xy* apart from the left and *xy* apart from the right border. So, width equals SIZE − 2*xy. The same holds for height. Each square is *xy* apart from the top and from the bottom.

The recursive method will require an *xy* parameter as discussed above and a parameter *group* to hold the circles.

```java
import javafx.application.Application;
import javafx.scene.Group;
import javafx.scene.Scene;
import javafx.scene.paint.Color;
import javafx.scene.shape.Rectangle;
import javafx.stage.Stage;

public class ConcentricSquares extends Application
{
    public final int SIZE = 300;
    public final int DIST = 20;

    public void squaresRec(int xy, Group group)
    {
        Rectangle rect;
        Color color = Color.NAVY;
        if (xy < SIZE/2)
        {
            rect = new Rectangle(xy, xy, SIZE-2*xy, SIZE-2*xy);
            rect.setFill(null);
            rect.setStrokeWidth(3);
            rect.setStroke(color);
            group.getChildren().add( rect);
            squaresRec(xy + DIST, group);
        }
    }

    public void start(Stage stage) throws Exception
    {
        Group group = new Group();
        Scene scene = new Scene(group, SIZE, SIZE, Color.PINK);
        squaresRec(DIST, group);
        stage.setTitle("Concentric Squares");
        stage.setScene(scene);
        stage.show();
    }
}
```

```
    public static void main(String[] args)
    {
        launch(args);
    }
}
```

 5) Draw concentric circles as shown. The largest circle has diameter equal to SIZE, which is equal to the width and height of the window. Each next circle is DIST apart from the previous one.

This is similar to example of concentric squares. The difference is that class Circle requires x,y parameters for the circles center as opposed to upper left corner in case of square. In addition, circle objects are specified by its radius, while rectangle requires the length of its width and height.

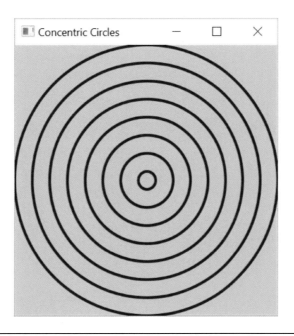

```
import javafx.application.Application;
import javafx.scene.Group;
import javafx.scene.Scene;
import javafx.scene.paint.Color;
import javafx.scene.shape.*;
import javafx.stage.Stage;

public class ConcentricCircles extends Application
{
    public final int SIZE = 300;
    public final int DIST = 20;
```

122

```
    public void circlesRec(int radius, Group group)
    {
        Circle circle;
        Color color = Color.NAVY;
        if (radius > 0)
        {
            circle = new Circle( SIZE/2, SIZE/2, radius);
            circle.setFill(null);
            circle.setStrokeWidth(3);
            circle.setStroke(color);
            group.getChildren().add( circle);
            circlesRec(radius  -  DIST, group);
        }
    }

    public void start(Stage stage) throws Exception
    {
        Group group = new Group();
        Scene scene = new Scene(group, SIZE, SIZE, Color.PINK);
        circlesRec(SIZE/2-DIST, group);
        stage.setTitle("Concentric Circles");
        stage.setScene(scene);
        stage.show();
    }

    public static void main(String[] args)
    {
        launch(args);
    }
}
```

6) Draw concentric squares filled with two alternating colors. Fill the largest square with the first color, and fill the next square with the second color. Each square is DIST apart from all four sides of the previous larger square. The sides of each square are 2*DIST shorter than the sides of its predecessor.

Since x and y are the same, only one formal parameter, which we call xy, is needed for both x and y. Width and height are also the same since we are drawing squares, and both can be determined, as discussed in the previous example, as function of SIZE and xy. Both width and height areequal to SIZE - 2*xy. The recursive method will need parameter xy and parameter *group*. Recursive method has stopping case when the upper left corner of the rectangle becomes larger than SIZE/2. In such a case, nothing needs to be done. Otherwise, the color should be the opposite of what it is currently to alternate colors at each next level of recursion. After that, a square with an upper left corner at *xy*, *xy* and width and height equal to SIZE – 2*xy is drawn. Finally, recursive subproblem with *xy* increased by DIST is invoked to draw the remaining squares filled with alternating colors.

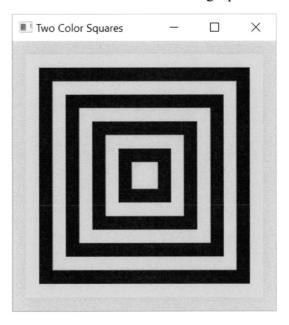

```java
import javafx.application.Application;
import javafx.scene.Group;
import javafx.scene.Scene;
import javafx.scene.paint.Color;
import javafx.scene.shape.*;
import javafx.stage.Stage;

public class TwoColorSquares extends Application
{
    public final int SIZE = 300;
    public final int DIST = 15;

    public void squaresRec(int xy, int n, Group group)
    {
        Rectangle rect;
        Color color;
        if (xy < SIZE/2)
        {
            if(n%2 == 0)
                color = Color.YELLOW;
            else
                color = Color.NAVY;
            rect = new Rectangle(xy, xy, SIZE-2*xy, SIZE-2*xy);
```

```
            rect.setFill(color);
            group.getChildren().add( rect);
            squaresRec(xy + DIST, n+1, group);
        }
    }

    public void start(Stage stage) throws Exception
    {
        Group group = new Group();
        Scene scene = new Scene(group, SIZE, SIZE,
                                Color.LIGHTGREY);
        squaresRec(DIST, 0, group);
        stage.setTitle("Two Color Squares");
        stage.setScene(scene);
        stage.show();
    }

    public static void main(String[] args)
    {
        launch(args);
    }
}
```

 7) Draw concentric circles filled with three alternating colors. Each circle is DIST apart from previous larger circle. The largest circle touches window in four points.

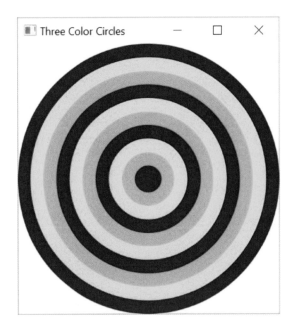

Circles require *x* and *y* for the center and *radius* as input parameters. Our circles are concentric and centered in the center of window which is SIZE/2, SIZE/2 for all pairs *x* and *y*, and we do not need them as parameter. Starting radius will be SIZE/2. If current circle has radius equal to *radius*, the adjacent smaller circle has radius equal to *radius* – DIST. The recursive method will need parameter *radius,* int parameter *n,* and parameter *group* to hold all circles. At the highest level of recursion, the stopping case is when radius is no longer positive. In such a case, nothing needs to be done. If *radius* is positive the current color should be determined based on *n* modulo 3. After that, a circle with current *radius* and color is created and added to the group. Finally, we call the recursive subproblem with *radius* decreased by DIST, n increased by one, and the same *group* parameter.

```java
import javafx.application.Application;
import javafx.scene.Group;
import javafx.scene.Scene;
import javafx.scene.paint.Color;
import javafx.scene.shape.*;
import javafx.stage.Stage;

public class ThreeColorCircles extends Application
{
    public final int SIZE = 300;
    public final int DIST = 15;

    public void circlesRec(int radius, int n, Group group)
    {
        Circle circle;
        Color color;
        if (radius > 0)
        {
            if(n%3 == 0)
                color = Color.BLUE;
            else if (n%3 == 1)
                color = Color.YELLOW;
            else
                color = Color.ORANGE;
            circle = new Circle( SIZE/2, SIZE/2, radius);
            circle.setFill(color);
            group.getChildren().add( circle);
            circlesRec(radius - DIST, n+1, group);
        }
    }

    public void start(Stage stage) throws Exception
    {
```

```
        Group group = new Group();
        Scene scene = new Scene(group, SIZE, SIZE,
                              Color.WHITE);
        circlesRec(SIZE/2, 0, group);
        stage.setTitle("Three Color Circles");
        stage.setScene(scene);
        stage.show();
    }

    public static void main(String[] args)
    {
        launch(args);
    }
}
```

8) Draw rectangles filled with purple color that gradually decrease in width. The largest is DIST apart from the top, left, right, and from the next adjacent rectangle bellow it. Each rectangle has height equal to DIST, and each next one has its width reduced by 2*DIST.

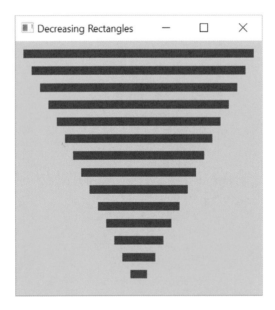

The recursive method has three formal parameters: *x*, *y* coordinates of the upper left corner of the rectangle, and group. Recursion stops when *x* is larger than SIZE/2. Otherwise, it creates a rectangle with upper left corner at x and y filled with purple color, and invokes the recursive method.

```java
import javafx.application.Application;
import javafx.scene.Group;
import javafx.scene.Scene;
import javafx.scene.paint.Color;
import javafx.scene.shape.*;
import javafx.stage.Stage;

public class DecreasingRectangles extends Application
{
    public final int SIZE = 300;
    public final int DIST = 10;

    public void rectanglesRec(int x, int y, Group group)
    {
        Rectangle rect;
        Color color = Color.PURPLE;
        if (x < SIZE/2)
        {
            rect = new Rectangle(x, y, SIZE - 2*x, DIST);
            rect.setFill(color);
            group.getChildren().add( rect);
            rectanglesRec(x + DIST, y + 2*DIST, group);
        }
    }

    public void start(Stage stage) throws Exception
    {
        Group group = new Group();
        Scene scene = new Scene(group, SIZE, SIZE, Color.PINK);
        rectanglesRec(DIST, DIST, group);
        stage.setTitle("Decreasing Rectangles");
        stage.setScene(scene);
        stage.show();
    }

    public static void main(String[] args)
    {
        launch(args);
    }
}
```

Several variations of squares

In examples 9–13 we draw variations of squares by calling four recursive subproblems. Variations are obtained by:

- interchanging the order of calling the method to create and draw one square, and calling the four recursive methods;
- calling the method to draw the outline of a square instead of filling it with color;
- and finally, using multiple colors at different levels of recursion.

 9) Draw squares filled with single color as shown.

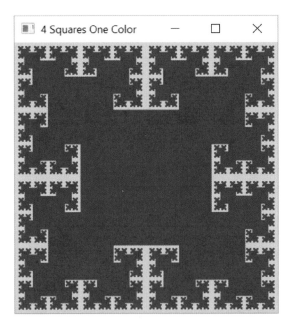

For each square, draw four smaller squares. The center of each smaller squares is one of the corners of the original square. The size of each of the smaller squares is ½ that of the size of the original square. Stopping case is when width and height (parameter n) fall below a given limit.

```java
import javafx.application.Application;
import javafx.scene.Group;
import javafx.scene.Scene;
import javafx.scene.paint.Color;
import javafx.scene.shape.*;
import javafx.stage.Stage;

public class OneColorFourSquares extends Application
{
    private final int SIZE = 300;
    private final int LIMIT = 1;
```

```java
// returns a square with side length n, and centered at x,y.
public Rectangle square(int x, int y, int n)
{
   return new Rectangle(x-n/2, y-n/2, n, n);
}

public void recSquares(int x, int y, int n, Group g)
{
   Rectangle rect;
   Color color = Color.PURPLE;
   if ( n > LIMIT)
   {
       rect = square(x, y, n);
       rect.setFill(color);
       g.getChildren().add(rect);
       recSquares(x-n/2, y+n/2, n/2, g);
       recSquares(x+n/2, y+n/2, n/2, g);
       recSquares(x+n/2, y-n/2, n/2, g);
       recSquares(x-n/2, y-n/2, n/2, g);
   }
}

public void start(Stage stage) throws Exception
{
       Group group = new Group();
       Scene scene = new Scene(group, SIZE, SIZE,
                              Color.LIGHTGREY);
       recSquares(SIZE/2, SIZE/2, SIZE/3, group);
       stage.setTitle(" 4 Squares One Color");
       stage.setScene(scene);
       stage.show();
   }

  public static void main(String[] args)
  {
       launch(args);
  }
}
```

 10) This example is similar to example 9. The difference is that in the previous example, the squares were filled with color, while in this case, only the outline of the squares is drawn.

Pictures show two examples with different base cases. In the left picture LIMIT is 10, while in the right one LIMIT is 3. Reducing the depth of recursive calls (by using larger LIMIT) makes the picture easier to understand.

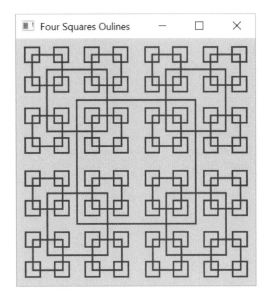 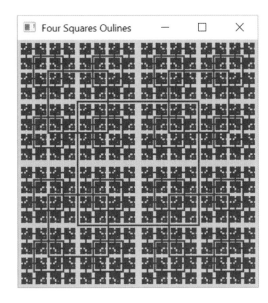

```java
import javafx.application.Application;
import javafx.scene.Group;
import javafx.scene.Scene;
import javafx.scene.paint.Color;
import javafx.scene.shape.*;
import javafx.stage.Stage;

public class FourSquaresOutline extends Application
{
    private final int SIZE = 300;
    private final int LIMIT = 3;

    //returns square with side n, and center at x,y.
    public Rectangle square(int x, int y, int n)
    {
        return new Rectangle(x-n/2, y-n/2, n, n);
    }

    public void recSquares(int x, int y, int n, Group g)
    {
        Rectangle rect;
        Color color = Color.PURPLE;
        if ( n > LIMIT)
```

```
        {
            rect = square(x, y, n);
            rect.setFill(null);
            rect.setStrokeWidth(2);
            rect.setStroke(color);
            g.getChildren().add(rect);
            recSquares(x-n/2, y+n/2, n/2, g);
            recSquares(x+n/2, y+n/2, n/2, g);
            recSquares(x+n/2, y-n/2, n/2, g);
            recSquares(x-n/2, y-n/2, n/2, g);
        }
    }

    public void start(Stage stage) throws Exception
    {
        Group group = new Group();
        Scene scene = new Scene(group, SIZE, SIZE,
                                Color.LIGHTGREY);
        recSquares(SIZE/2, SIZE/2, SIZE/3, group);
        stage.setTitle(" Four Squares Oulines");
        stage.setScene(scene);
        stage.show();
    }

    public static void main(String[] args)
    {
        launch(args);
    }
}
```

 11) Modify example 9 to fill the interior of all squares but use two colors (black and magenta) in alternating levels of recursion.

This can be achieved by adding one more integer parameter *k* in the recursive method. Color is set to magenta if *k* is even, and is black, otherwise. The parameter *k* is increased by one at each level of recursion. The recursive method will have the following parameters: *x* and *y* coordinates of the center of the square, *n* length of a side, *k* to alternate colors, and *group* parameter.

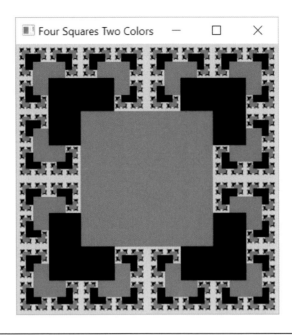

```
import javafx.application.Application;
import javafx.scene.Group;
import javafx.scene.Scene;
import javafx.scene.paint.Color;
import javafx.scene.shape.*;
import javafx.stage.Stage;

public class FourSquaresTwoColors extends Application
{
    private final int SIZE = 300;
    private final int LIMIT = 1;

    // returns a square with side equal to n, and centered at x,y.
    public Rectangle square(int x, int y, int n)
    {
        return new Rectangle(x-n/2, y-n/2, n, n);
    }

    public void recSquares(int x, int y, int n, int k, Group g)
    {
        Rectangle rect;
        Color color ;
        if ( n > LIMIT)
        {
            recSquares(x-n/2, y+n/2, n/2, k+1, g);
            recSquares(x+n/2, y+n/2, n/2, k+1, g);
```

```
              recSquares(x+n/2, y-n/2, n/2, k+1, g);
              recSquares(x-n/2, y-n/2, n/2, k+1, g);
              rect = square(x, y, n);
              if (k % 2 == 0)
                 color = Color.MAGENTA;
              else
                 color = Color.BLACK;
              rect.setFill(color);
              g.getChildren().add(rect);
       }
   }

   public void start(Stage stage) throws Exception
   {
         Group group = new Group();
         Scene scene = new Scene(group, SIZE, SIZE,
                                 Color.LIGHTGREY);
         recSquares(SIZE/2, SIZE/2, SIZE/2, 0, group);
         stage.setTitle("Four Squares Two Colors");
         stage.setScene(scene);
         stage.show();
   }

   public static void main(String[] args)
   {
         launch(args);
   }
}
```

 12) Draw squares as in example 11 so that largest square is drawn first and smallest ones are drwn last.

The difference between example 11 and this one is in the order of drawing a square and making four recursive calls. In example 11 the four recursive calls are made before calling the method to draw a large square. In this example, the four recursive calls are made after drawing the square. The largest square looks as if it is behind all of the other squares. That is because it is done first. In both examples we use black and magenta colors at alternating levels to fill the squares.

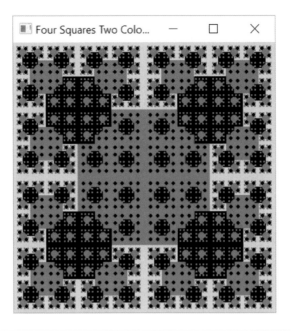

```java
import javafx.application.Application;
import javafx.scene.Group;
import javafx.scene.Scene;
import javafx.scene.paint.Color;
import javafx.scene.shape.*;
import javafx.stage.Stage;

public class FourSquares2ColorsReversed extends Application
{
    private final int SIZE = 300;
    private final int LIMIT = 1;

    // returns a square with side equal to n, and centered at
x,y.
    public Rectangle square(int x, int y, int n)
    {
      return new Rectangle(x-n/2, y-n/2, n, n);
    }

    public void recSquares(int x, int y, int n, int k, Group g)
    {
      Rectangle rect;
      Color color ;
      if ( n > LIMIT)
      {
          rect = square(x, y, n);
```

```
            if (k % 2 == 0)
                color = Color.MAGENTA;
            else
                color = Color.BLACK;
            rect.setFill(color);
            g.getChildren().add(rect);
            recSquares(x-n/2, y+n/2, n/2, k+1, g);
            recSquares(x+n/2, y+n/2, n/2, k+1, g);
            recSquares(x+n/2, y-n/2, n/2, k+1, g);
            recSquares(x-n/2, y-n/2, n/2, k+1, g);
        }
    }

    public void start(Stage stage) throws Exception
    {
        Group group = new Group();
        Scene scene = new Scene(group, SIZE, SIZE,
                               Color.LIGHTGREY);
        recSquares(SIZE/2, SIZE/2, SIZE/2, 0, group);
        stage.setTitle("Four Squares Two Colors Reversed");
        stage.setScene(scene);
        stage.show();
    }

    public static void main(String[] args)
    {
        launch(args);
    }
}
```

 13) This example shown below is obtained from example 11 by using five alternating colors instead of two and making the background black.

All squares of the same size have the same color which is achieved by using the same color at each of the four recursive calls.

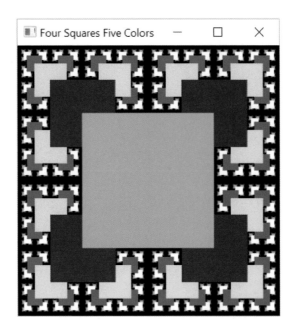

```
import javafx.application.Application;
import javafx.scene.Group;
import javafx.scene.Scene;
import javafx.scene.paint.Color;
import javafx.scene.shape.*;
import javafx.stage.Stage;

public class FourSquaresFiveColors extends Application
{
    private final int SIZE = 300;
    private final int LIMIT = 1;

    // returns a square with side equal n, and centered at x,y.
    public Rectangle square(int x, int y, int n)
    {
      return new Rectangle(x-n/2, y-n/2, n, n);
    }

    public void recSquares(int x, int y, int n, int k, Group g)
    {
      Rectangle rect;
      Color color = null;
      if ( n > LIMIT)
      {
          recSquares(x-n/2, y+n/2, n/2, k+1, g);
```

```
            recSquares(x+n/2, y+n/2, n/2, k+1, g);
            recSquares(x+n/2, y-n/2, n/2, k+1, g);
            recSquares(x-n/2, y-n/2, n/2, k+1, g);
            rect = square(x, y, n);
            if ( k%5 == 0 )
               color = Color.CYAN;
            else if (k%5 == 1)
               color = Color.BLUE;
            else if (k%5 == 2)
               color = Color.YELLOW;
            else if (k%5 == 3)
               color = Color.GREEN;
            else if (k%5 == 4)
               color = Color.WHITE;
            rect.setFill(color);
            g.getChildren().add(rect);
      }
   }

   public void start(Stage stage) throws Exception
   {
        Group group = new Group();
        Scene scene = new Scene(group, SIZE, SIZE,
Color.BLACK);
        recSquares(SIZE/2, SIZE/2, SIZE/2, 0, group);
        stage.setTitle("Four Squares Five Colors");
        stage.setScene(scene);
        stage.show();
   }

   public static void main(String[] args)
   {
        launch(args);
   }
}
```

14) Draw the snowflake as shown.

Start with three lines that make an equilateral triangle. For each of those three lines do the following. At the next level replace a line with four lines. Each of the four lines has length equal to 1/3 of the length of the original line. The first and fourth lines are placed on the first and last third of the original line. The second and third line make a smaller equilateral triangle with the missing middle third of the original line. The transformation of the horizontal line within the first four levels of recursion is given below.

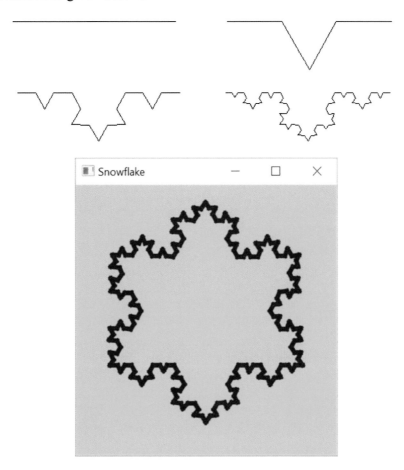

```
import javafx.application.Application;
import javafx.scene.Group;
import javafx.scene.Scene;
import javafx.scene.paint.Color;
import javafx.scene.shape.*;
import javafx.stage.Stage;

public class Snowflake extends Application
{
    private final double SQ = Math.sqrt(3)/6;
    private final int SIZE = 300;

    public void recflake (int x1, int y1, int x5,int y5,
                          Group g, int level)
    {
        Line line;
```

```java
        int dx, dy, x2, y2, x3, y3, x4, y4;
        if ( level==1)
        {
            line = new Line(x1, y1, x5, y5);
            line.setStrokeWidth(5);
            line.setStroke(Color.NAVY);
            g.getChildren().add( line);
        }
        else
        {
          dx=x5-x1;
          dy=y5-y1;
          x2=x1+dx/3;
          y2=y1+dy/3;
          x3=(int)((x1+x5)/2 - SQ*(y1-y5));
          y3=(int)((y1+y5)/2 - SQ*(x5-x1));
          x4=x1+2*dx/3;
          y4=y1+2*dy/3;

            recflake(x1, y1, x2, y2, g, level-1);
            recflake(x2, y2, x3, y3, g, level-1);
            recflake(x3, y3, x4, y4, g, level-1);
            recflake(x4, y4, x5, y5, g, level-1);
        }
    }

    public void start(Stage stage) throws Exception
    {
        Group g = new Group();
        Scene scene = new Scene(g, SIZE, SIZE, Color.PINK);
        recflake(SIZE-40, 2*SIZE/3, 40, 2*SIZE/3, g, 4);
        recflake(SIZE/2, 20, SIZE-40, 2*SIZE/3, g, 4);
        recflake(40, 2*SIZE/3, SIZE/2, 20, g, 4);
        stage.setTitle("Snowflake");
        stage.setScene(scene);
        stage.show();
    }

    public static void main(String[] args)
    {
        launch(args);
    }
}
```

15) Draw Inverted Snowflake example as shown. The difference between Snowflake and Inverted Snowflake is that the two inner lines are drawn inward for inverted Snowflake, and for Snowflake they were drawn outward.

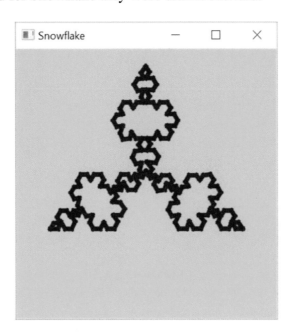

```
import javafx.application.Application;
import javafx.scene.Group;
import javafx.scene.Scene;
import javafx.scene.paint.Color;
import javafx.scene.shape.*;
import javafx.stage.Stage;

public class InvertedSnowflake extends Application
{
    private final double SQ = Math.sqrt(3)/6;
    private final int SIZE = 300;

    public void recflake (int x1, int y1, int x5,int y5,
                          Group g, int level)
    {
        Line line;
        int dx, dy, x2, y2, x3, y3, x4, y4;
        if ( level==1)
        {
            line = new Line(x1, y1, x5, y5);
```

```
                        line.setStrokeWidth(5);
                        line.setStroke(Color.NAVY);
                        g.getChildren().add( line);
                }
            else
            {
                dx=x5-x1;
                dy=y5-y1;
                x2=x1+dx/3;
                y2=y1+dy/3;
                x3=(int)((x1+x5)/2 + SQ*(y1-y5));
                y3=(int)((y1+y5)/2 + SQ*(x5-x1));
                x4=x1+2*dx/3;
                y4=y1+2*dy/3;

                recflake(x1, y1, x2, y2, g, level-1);
                recflake(x2, y2, x3, y3, g, level-1);
                recflake(x3, y3, x4, y4, g, level-1);
                recflake(x4, y4, x5, y5, g, level-1);
            }
    }

    public void start(Stage stage) throws Exception
    {
            Group g = new Group();
            Scene scene = new Scene(g, SIZE, SIZE, Color.PINK);
            recflake(SIZE-40, 2*SIZE/3, 40, 2*SIZE/3, g, 4);
            recflake(SIZE/2, 20, SIZE-40, 2*SIZE/3, g, 4);
            recflake(40, 2*SIZE/3, SIZE/2, 20, g, 4);
            stage.setTitle("Snowflake");
            stage.setScene(scene);
            stage.show();
    }

    public static void main(String[] args)
    {
            launch(args);
    }
}
```

16) Draw circles as shown. At each level draw one large circle and make four recursive calls to draw four smaller circles that are tangent to the original circle and positioned on the east, south, west and north of it.

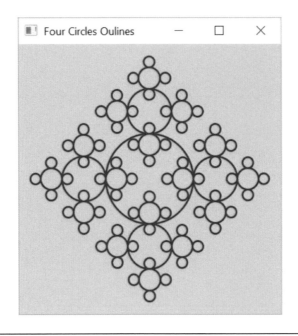

```java
import javafx.application.Application;
import javafx.scene.Group;
import javafx.scene.Scene;
import javafx.scene.paint.Color;
import javafx.scene.shape.*;
import javafx.stage.Stage;

public class FourCirclesOutline extends Application
{
    private final int SIZE = 300;
    private final int LIMIT = 3;

    public void recCircles(int x, int y, int r, Group g)
    {
      Circle circle;
      Color color = Color.PURPLE;
      if ( r > LIMIT)
      {
          circle = new Circle(x, y, r);
          circle.setFill(null);
          circle.setStrokeWidth(2);
          circle.setStroke(color);
          g.getChildren().add(circle);
          recCircles(x-3*r/2, y, r/2, g);
          recCircles(x, y+3*r/2, r/2, g);
          recCircles(x+3*r/2, y, r/2, g);
```

```
            recCircles(x, y-3*r/2, r/2, g);
        }
    }

    public void start(Stage stage) throws Exception
    {
        Group group = new Group();
        Scene scene = new Scene(group, SIZE, SIZE,
Color.LIGHTGREY);
        recCircles(SIZE/2, SIZE/2, SIZE/6, group);
        stage.setTitle(" Four Circles Oulines");
        stage.setScene(scene);
        stage.show();
    }

    public static void main(String[] args)
    {
        launch(args);
    }
}
```

17) Draw circles as shown below.

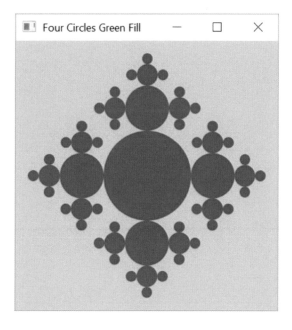

The difference between the examples 16 and 17 is that example 16 draws outlines of circles and example 17 draws the same but filled with green color.

```java
import javafx.application.Application;
import javafx.application.Application;
import javafx.scene.Group;
import javafx.scene.Scene;
import javafx.scene.paint.Color;
import javafx.scene.shape.*;
import javafx.stage.Stage;

public class FourCirclesGreen extends Application
{
   private final int SIZE = 300;
   private final int LIMIT = 3;

   public void recCircles(int x, int y, int r, Group g)
   {
     Circle circle;
     Color color = Color.GREEN;
     if ( r > LIMIT)
     {
         circle = new Circle(x, y, r);
         circle.setFill(color);
         g.getChildren().add(circle);
         recCircles(x-3*r/2, y, r/2, g);
         recCircles(x, y+3*r/2, r/2, g);
         recCircles(x+3*r/2, y, r/2, g);
         recCircles(x, y-3*r/2, r/2, g);
     }
   }

   public void start(Stage stage) throws Exception
   {
         Group group = new Group();
         Scene scene = new Scene(group, SIZE, SIZE,
Color.LIGHTGREY);
         recCircles(SIZE/2, SIZE/2, SIZE/6, group);
         stage.setTitle(" Four Circles Green Fill");
         stage.setScene(scene);
         stage.show();
    }

    public static void main(String[] args)
    {
         launch(args);
    }
}
```

18) Draw circles as shown in the picture below. This example uses three different colors (red, yellow, and green) for various levels of recursion.

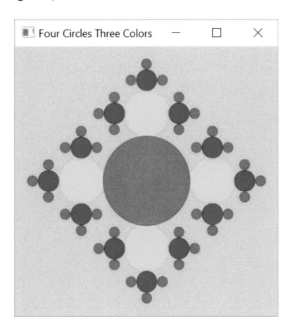

```java
import javafx.application.Application;
import javafx.scene.Group;
import javafx.scene.Scene;
import javafx.scene.paint.Color;
import javafx.scene.shape.*;
import javafx.stage.Stage;

public class FourCirclesThreeColors extends Application
{
    private final int SIZE = 300;
    private final int LIMIT = 3;

    public void recCircles(int x, int y, int r, int k, Group g)
    {
      Circle circle;
      Color color;
      if ( r > LIMIT)
      {
          recCircles(x-3*r/2, y, r/2, k+1, g);
          recCircles(x, y+3*r/2, r/2, k+1, g);
          recCircles(x+3*r/2, y, r/2, k+1, g);
          recCircles(x, y-3*r/2, r/2, k+1, g);
```

```
            if(k%3 == 0)
                color = Color.RED;
            else if (k%3 == 1)
                color = Color.YELLOW;
            else
                color = Color.GREEN;

            circle = new Circle(x, y, r);
            circle.setFill(color);
            g.getChildren().add(circle);
        }
    }

    public void start(Stage stage) throws Exception
    {
        Group group = new Group();
        Scene scene = new Scene(group, SIZE, SIZE,
                                Color.LIGHTGREY);
        recCircles(SIZE/2, SIZE/2, SIZE/6, 0, group);
        stage.setTitle("Four Circles Three Colors");
        stage.setScene(scene);
        stage.show();
    }

    public static void main(String[] args)
    {
        launch(args);
    }
}
```

 19) In this example the four circles are not tangent on the original circle. They are partially overlapped by the large circle as shown. They are drawn north, east, south and west of the main circle and their size is one half of the size of the larger circle.

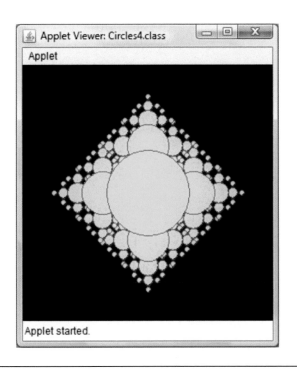

```java
import javax.swing.*;
import java.awt.*;

public class Circles4 extends JApplet
{
    private final int SIZE = 300;
    private Color colortype = Color.yellow;

    // draw circle centered in x,y with radius r.
    public void drawCircle(int x, int y, int r, Graphics g)
    {
      g.fillOval(x-r, y-r, r*2, r*2);
      g.setColor(Color.red);              // red border around the circle
      g.drawOval(x-r, y-r, r*2, r*2);
    }

    public void recursiveCircles (int x, int y, int r, Graphics
                                     g)
    {
      if ( r > 1)
      {
        recursiveCircles(x-r-5, y, r/2, g);
        recursiveCircles(x, y+r+5, r/2, g);
        recursiveCircles(x+r+5, y, r/2, g);
```

142

```
            recursiveCircles(x, y-r-5, r/2, g);
            g.setColor(colortype);
            drawCircle(x, y, r, g);
        }
    }

    public void paint(Graphics g)
    {
        g.fillRect(0, 0, SIZE, SIZE);
        recursiveCircles (SIZE/2, SIZE/2, SIZE/6, g);
    }
}
```

20) In this example eight circles are drawn at each level to overlap with the main circle as shown.

The main circle is drawn after invoking the eight recursive calls. Eight recursive calls draw eight smaller circles positioned east, west, south, north, south-east, southwest, north-east, and northwest of the current circle.

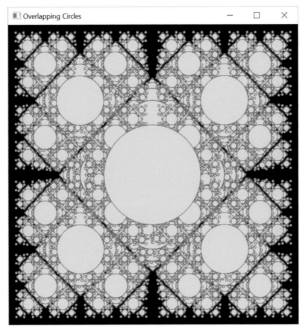

```
import javafx.application.Application;
import javafx.scene.Group;
import javafx.scene.Scene;
import javafx.scene.paint.Color;
import javafx.scene.shape.*;
```

```java
import javafx.stage.Stage;

public class OverlappingCirles extends Application
{
    private final int SIZE = 500;
    private final int LIMIT = 1;

    public void recCircles(int x, int y, int r, Group g)
    {
      Circle circle;
      if ( r > LIMIT)
      {
          recCircles(x-r, y, r/2, g);
          recCircles(x, y+r, r/2, g);
          recCircles(x+r, y, r/2, g);
          recCircles(x, y-r, r/2, g);
          recCircles(x-3*r/2, y-3*r/2, r/2, g);
          recCircles(x-3*r/2, y+3*r/2, r/2, g);
          recCircles(x+3*r/2, y+3*r/2, r/2, g);
          recCircles(x+3*r/2, y-3*r/2, r/2, g);
          circle = new Circle(x, y, r);
          circle.setFill(Color.YELLOW);
          g.getChildren().add(circle);
          circle = new Circle(x, y, r);
          circle.setFill(null);
          circle.setStrokeWidth(1);
          circle.setStroke(Color.RED);
          g.getChildren().add(circle);
      }
    }

    public void start(Stage stage) throws Exception
    {
       Group group = new Group();
       Scene scene = new Scene(group, SIZE, SIZE, Color.BLACK);
       recCircles(SIZE/2, SIZE/2, SIZE/6, group);
       stage.setTitle("Overlapping Circles");
       stage.setScene(scene);
       stage.show();
    }

    public static void main(String[] args)
    {
        launch(args);
    }
}
```

21-22) To draw a C-curve as shown, start with the two points that form a vertical line. Instead of drawing that line replace the line with two shorter lines that both have equal length and make a right angle triangle such that the original line would have been the hypotenuse. Lines are only drawn when *level* is 1. The first few levels for the C-curve are as follows.

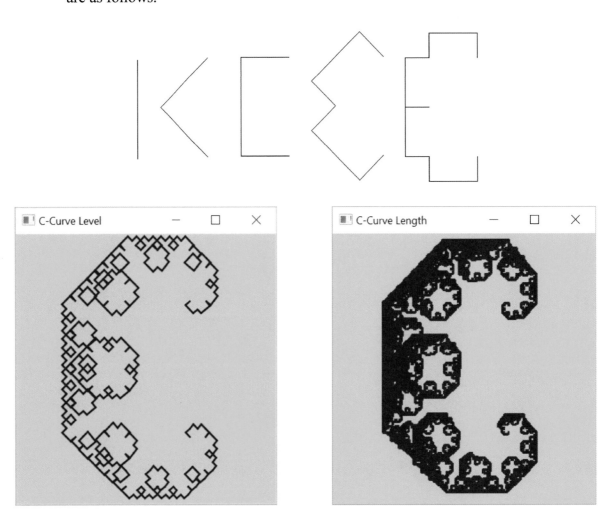

The left picture shows the result for implementation where we invoke recursion with depth level 10, and the right one shows the result for implementation where we stop when the length of the line is less or equal to 1 .

IMPLEMENTATION 1

```
import javafx.application.Application;
import javafx.scene.Group;
import javafx.scene.Scene;
import javafx.scene.paint.Color;
import javafx.scene.shape.*;
import javafx.stage.Stage;
```

```
public class C_Curve extends Application
{
    public final int SIZE = 300;

    public void recLines(int x1, int y1, int x2, int y2,
                         Group group, int level)
    {
        Line line;
        int x3,y3;
        if (level == 1)
        {
            line = new Line(x1, y1, x2, y2);
            line.setStrokeWidth(2);
            line.setStroke(Color.NAVY);
            group.getChildren().add( line);
        }
        else
        {
            x3 = (int) ((x1+x2)/2.0 + (y1-y2)/2.0);
            y3 = (int) ((y1+y2)/2.0 + (x2-x1)/2.0);
            recLines(x1, y1, x3, y3, group, level-1);
            recLines(x3, y3, x2, y2, group, level-1);
        }
    }

    public void start(Stage stage) throws Exception
    {
        Group group = new Group();
        Scene scene = new Scene(group, SIZE, SIZE, Color.PINK);
        recLines(2*SIZE/3, SIZE/4,2*SIZE/3, SIZE-SIZE/4, group,
                 10);
        stage.setTitle("C-Curve Level");
        stage.setScene(scene);
        stage.show();
    }

    public static void main(String[] args)
    {
        launch(args);
    }
}
```

For a small distance between the two starting points and a large number for level, the above algorithm may become very inefficient since it will draw the same lines over and over until it reaches stopping case.

IMPLEMENTATION 2

```java
import javafx.application.Application;
import javafx.scene.Group;
import javafx.scene.Scene;
import javafx.scene.paint.Color;
import javafx.scene.shape.*;
import javafx.stage.Stage;

public class C_Curve_Length extends Application
{
    public final int SIZE = 300;
    public final int LENGTH = 1;

    public void recLines(int x1, int y1, int x2, int y2,
                          Group g)
    {
        Line line;
        int x3, y3;
        if ((x1-x2)*(x1-x2) + (y1-y2)*(y1-y2) <= LENGTH)
        {
            line = new Line(x1, y1, x2, y2);
            line.setStrokeWidth(2);
            line.setStroke(Color.NAVY);
            g.getChildren().add( line);
        }
        else
        {
            x3 = (int) ((x1+x2)/2.0 + (y1-y2)/2.0);
            y3 = (int) ((y1+y2)/2.0 + (x2-x1)/2.0);
            recLines(x1, y1, x3, y3, g);
            recLines(x3, y3, x2, y2, g);
        }
    }

    public void start(Stage stage) throws Exception
    {
        Group group = new Group();
        Scene scene = new Scene(group, SIZE, SIZE, Color.PINK);
        recLines(2*SIZE/3, 80, 2*SIZE/3, SIZE-80, group);
        stage.setTitle("C-Curve Length");
        stage.setScene(scene);
        stage.show();
    }
```

```
    public static void main(String[] args)
    {
        launch(args);
    }
}
```

23) We draw the dragon curve in a similar way as we did the C curve, except that for each next adjacent line we change the direction of drawing the two smaller lines. The first five levels of Dragon curve are shown below.

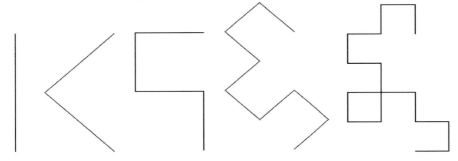

The two pictures show the same recursive method called starting with level 8 and level 14, respectively.

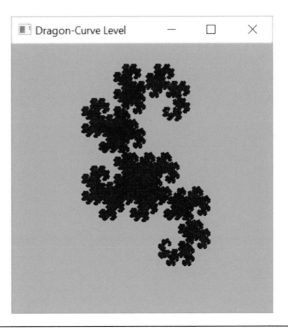

```
import javafx.application.Application;
import javafx.scene.Group;
import javafx.scene.Scene;
```

```java
import javafx.scene.paint.Color;
import javafx.scene.shape.*;
import javafx.stage.Stage;

public class DragonCurve extends Application
{
    public final int SIZE = 300;

    public void recLines(int x1, int y1, int x2, int y2, Group
                          group, int level, boolean direction)
    {
        Line line;
        int x3,y3;
        if (level == 1)
        {
            line = new Line(x1, y1, x2, y2);
            line.setStrokeWidth(2);
            line.setStroke(Color.NAVY);
            group.getChildren().add( line);
        }
        else
        {
            if (direction)
            {
                x3 = (int) ((x1+x2)/2.0 + (y1-y2)/2.0);
                y3 = (int) ((y1+y2)/2.0 + (x2-x1)/2.0);
            }
            else
            {
                x3 = (int) ((x1+x2)/2.0 - (y1-y2)/2.0);
                y3 = (int) ((y1+y2)/2.0 - (x2-x1)/2.0);
            }
            recLines(x1, y1, x3, y3, group, level-1, true);
            recLines(x3, y3, x2, y2, group, level-1, false);
        }
    }

    public void start(Stage stage) throws Exception
    {
        Group group = new Group();
        Scene scene = new Scene(group, SIZE, SIZE,
                            Color.LIGHTGREEN);
        recLines(SIZE*3/5, SIZE/4, SIZE*3/5, SIZE-SIZE/4,
                group, 14, true);
        stage.setTitle("Dragon Curve");
```

```
            stage.setScene(scene);
            stage.show();
        }

    public static void main(String[] args)
        {
            launch(args);
        }
}
```

24 - 25) Draw concentric sectors with sweeping angle DELTA. Reduce diameter by DELTA/4 and fill the sectors with an alternating array of 10 colors. In the left picture, we stop after 360 degrees, and in the right picture, we stop after 2*360 degrees.

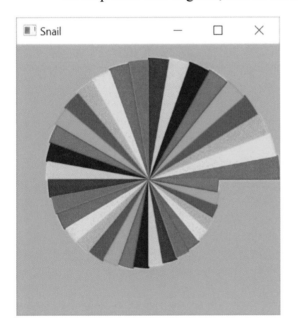 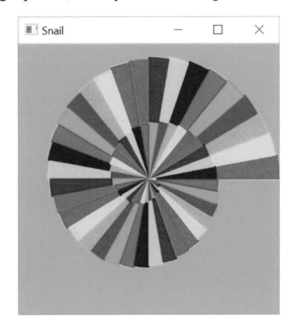

```
import javafx.application.Application;
import javafx.scene.Group;
import javafx.scene.Scene;
import javafx.scene.paint.Color;
import javafx.scene.shape.*;
import javafx.stage.Stage;

public class Snail extends Application
{
    private final int DELTA = 10;
    private final int SIZE = 300;
    private int i = -1;
```

```
   private Color[] c = {Color.RED, Color.YELLOW, Color.ORANGE,
                        Color.GREEN, Color.CYAN, Color.MAGENTA,
                        Color.BLUE, Color.PINK, Color.PURPLE,
                        Color.GRAY};

public void recSnail (int xy, int angle, Group g)
{
   Arc arc;
   if (angle < 360 ) // change to (angle<360*2) for ex 26)
   {
       if (i == 9)
          i = 0;
       else
          i=i+1;
       arc = new Arc(SIZE/2, SIZE/2, SIZE/2-xy, SIZE/2-xy, angle,
                     DELTA);
      arc.setType(ArcType.ROUND);
      arc.setStroke(c[i]);
      arc.setFill(c[i]);
      g.getChildren().add(arc);
      recSnail(xy + DELTA/4, angle + DELTA, g);
   }
}

public void start(Stage stage)
{
   Group group = new Group();
   Scene scene =new Scene(group, SIZE, SIZE, Color.LIGHTGREEN);
   recSnail(0, 0, group);
   stage.setTitle("Snail");
   stage.setScene(scene);
   stage.show();
}

public static void main(String[] args)
{
   launch(args);
}
}
```

 26) Design a recursive method to draw Sierpinski triangles as shown.

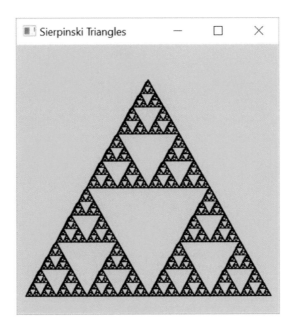

The recursive method has seven parameters. The first six are the three pairs of *x,y* coordinates of triangle corners, and the last one is *group*. At the highest level, draw three lines to connect every two of the three given points that make up the corners of the equilateral triangle. In addition, invoke three recursive calls. In each recursive call, the three pairs of *x,y* coordinates represent one of the corners of the current triangle and two midpoints on the two sides coming from that corner. The stopping case is when the length of the triangle side is below a given limit.

```java
import javafx.application.Application;
import javafx.scene.Group;
import javafx.scene.Scene;
import javafx.scene.paint.Color;
import javafx.scene.shape.*;
import javafx.stage.Stage;

public class SierpinskiTriangles extends Application
{
    private final int SIZE = 300;
    private final int DIST = 10;

    public void recTrg( int x1, int y1, int x2, int y2,
                        int x3,int y3, Group g)
    {
        Line l1, l2, l3;
        Group triangle;
        if (( (x1-x2)*(x1-x2) + (y1-y2)*(y1-y2)) > DIST )
        {
            l1 = new Line(x1, y1, x2, y2);
```

```
            l2 = new Line(x2, y2, x3, y3);
            l3 = new Line(x3, y3, x1, y1);
            triangle = new Group(l1, l2, l3);
            g.getChildren().add(triangle);
            recTrg((x1+x2)/2,(y1+y2)/2,(x1+x3)/2,(y1+y3)/2,
                    x1,y1,g);
            recTrg((x1+x2)/2,(y1+y2)/2,(x3+x2)/2,(y3+y2)/2,
                    x2,y2,g);
            recTrg((x1+x3)/2,(y1+y3)/2,(x3+x2)/2,(y3+y2)/2,
                    x3,y3,g);
        }
    }

    public void start(Stage stage)
    {
        Group group = new Group();
        Scene scene =new Scene(group, SIZE, SIZE, Color.PINK);
        recTrg(DIST, SIZE-2*DIST, SIZE-DIST, SIZE-2*DIST, SIZE/2,
               4*DIST, group);
        stage.setTitle("Sierpinski Triangles");
        stage.setScene(scene);
        stage.show();
    }

    public static void main(String[] args)
    {
        launch(args);
    }
}
```

 27) Draw stairs as shown. All stairs have width and height equal to DIST.

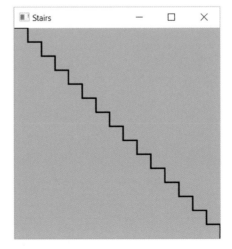

```java
import javafx.application.Application;
import javafx.scene.Group;
import javafx.scene.Scene;
import javafx.scene.paint.Color;
import javafx.scene.shape.*;
import javafx.stage.Stage;

public class Stairs extends Application
{
    public final int SIZE = 300;
    public final int DIST = 20;

    public void recStairs(int x, int y, Group g)
    {
      Line hLine, vLine;
      Group stair;
      if (x < SIZE)
      {
         hLine = new Line(x, y, x+DIST, y);  //horizontal part
         hLine.setStrokeWidth(2);
         vLine = new Line(x+DIST, y, x+DIST, y+DIST); //stair
                                     // vertical part
         vLine.setStrokeWidth(2);
         stair = new Group(vLine, hLine);
         g.getChildren().add(stair);
         recStairs(x+DIST, y+DIST, g);
      }
    }

    public void start(Stage stage)
    {
        Group group = new Group();
        Scene scene =new Scene(group, SIZE, SIZE,
                            Color.LIGHTGREEN);
        recStairs(0, 0, group);
        stage.setTitle("Stairs");
        stage.setScene(scene);
        stage.show();
    }

    public static void main(String[] args)
    {
        launch(args);
    }
}
```

28) Draw a spiral as shown. Each line is perpendicular to and shorter by DIST than the previous one.

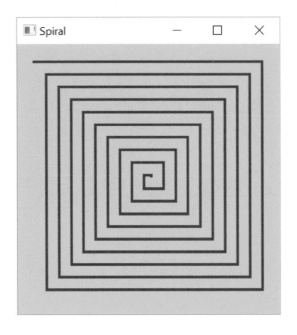

```java
import javafx.application.Application;
import javafx.scene.Group;
import javafx.scene.Scene;
import javafx.scene.paint.Color;
import javafx.scene.shape.*;
import javafx.stage.Stage;

public class Spiral extends Application
{
    private final int LIMIT = 7;
    private final int SIZE = 300;

    public void recSpiral(int x1, int y1, int x2, int y2,
                          int size, Group g)
    {
      int x3, y3;
      Line line;
      if ( size <= LIMIT)
      {
        line = new Line(x1,y1,x2,y2);
        line.setStroke(Color.PURPLE);
        line.setStrokeWidth(3);
        g.getChildren().add(line);
```

```
      }
      else
      {
        if (x1 == x2)
        {
          y3 = y2;
          if (y1 > y2)
            x3 = x2 + size - LIMIT;
          else
            x3 = x2 -(size - LIMIT);
        }
        else
        {
          x3 = x2;
          if (x1 < x2)
            y3 = y2 + (size - LIMIT);
          else
            y3 = y2 - (size - LIMIT);
        }
        recSpiral(x2, y2, x3, y3, size-LIMIT, g);
        line = new Line(x1, y1, x2, y2);
        line.setStroke(Color.PURPLE);
        line.setStrokeWidth(3);
        g.getChildren().add(line);
      }
   }

   public void start(Stage stage)
   {
       Group group = new Group();
       Scene scene =new Scene(group, SIZE, SIZE, Color.PINK);
       recSpiral(20, 20, SIZE-20, 20, SIZE-40, group);
       stage.setTitle("Spiral");
       stage.setScene(scene);
       stage.show();
   }

   public static void main(String[] args)
   {
       launch(args);
   }
}
```

29) To draw a tree, start with a vertical line. For each line draw three new lines that start at the top of the original line. Stop when the lines are small enough.

```java
import javafx.application.Application;
import javafx.scene.Group;
import javafx.scene.Scene;
import javafx.scene.paint.Color;
import javafx.scene.shape.*;
import javafx.stage.Stage;
import javafx.geometry.*;

public class Tree extends Application
{
  public final int SIZE = 300;
  public final double START_ANGLE = Math.PI / 2;
  public final double DELTA_ANGLE = Math.PI / 6;
  public final double REDUCTION = 0.7;
  public final int MINIMAL_LENGTH = 5;

  private int getNewX(int x, int y, double theta,
                      double length)
  {
    return (int)( length * Math.cos(theta)  + x );
  }

  private int getNewY(int x, int y, double theta,
                      double length)
```

```java
  {
    return  (int)( -length*Math.sin(theta) + y );
  }

  public void recTree (int x, int y, double theta, int length,
                       Group g)
  {
    if ( length > MINIMAL_LENGTH )
    {
      Group branches;
      int x1,y1;
      Line line1, line2, line3;
      x1 = getNewX(x, y, theta - DELTA_ANGLE, length);
      y1 = getNewY(x, y, theta - DELTA_ANGLE, length);
      line1 = new Line( x, y, x1, y1);
      line1.setStroke(Color.BROWN);
      line1.setStrokeWidth(2);
      recTree( x1, y1, theta-DELTA_ANGLE,
               (int)(length*REDUCTION), g);

      x1 = getNewX(x, y, theta, length);
      y1 = getNewY(x, y, theta, length);
      line2 = new Line( x, y, x1, y1);
      line2.setStroke(Color.BROWN);
      line2.setStrokeWidth(2);
      recTree( x1, y1, theta, (int)(length*REDUCTION), g);

      x1 = getNewX(x, y, theta + DELTA_ANGLE, length);
      y1 = getNewY(x, y, theta + DELTA_ANGLE, length);
      line3 = new Line( x, y, x1, y1);
      line3.setStroke(Color.BROWN);
      line3.setStrokeWidth(2);
      recTree( x1, y1, theta + DELTA_ANGLE,
               (int)(length*REDUCTION), g);

      branches = new Group(line1, line2, line3);
      g.getChildren().add(branches);
    }
  }

  public void start(Stage stage)
  {
    Group group = new Group();
    Line line = new Line(SIZE/2, SIZE-10, SIZE/2, 2*SIZE/3);
    line.setStrokeWidth(4);
```

```
        line.setStroke(Color.BROWN);
        group.getChildren().add(line);
        recTree(SIZE/2, 2*SIZE/3, START_ANGLE, SIZE/6,  group);
        Scene scene = new Scene(group, SIZE, SIZE,
                                Color.LIGHTGREEN);
        stage.setTitle("Tree Branch Factor 3");
        stage.setScene(scene);
        stage.show();
        }

        public static void main(String[] args)
        {
            launch(args);
        }
}
```

 30) To draw a broccoli, do the same as for drawing the tree. For each line draw three new lines that start at the top of the line. When the lines are small enough draw a circle in a lighter green color.

```
import javafx.application.Application;
import javafx.scene.Group;
import javafx.scene.Scene;
import javafx.scene.paint.Color;
```

```java
import javafx.scene.shape.*;
import javafx.stage.Stage;
import javafx.geometry.*;

public class Broccoli extends Application
{
  public final int SIZE = 300;
  public final double START_ANGLE = Math.PI / 2;
  public final double DELTA_ANGLE = Math.PI / 6;
  public final double REDUCTION = 0.7;
  public final int MINIMAL_LENGTH = 5;

  private int getNewX(int x, int y, double theta,
                      double length)
  {
    return (int)( length * Math.cos(theta)  + x );
  }

  private int getNewY(int x, int y, double theta,
                      double length)
  {
    return (int)( -length*Math.sin(theta) + y );
  }

  public void recTree (int x, int y, double theta, int length,
                       Group g)
  {
    if ( length > MINIMAL_LENGTH )
    {
      Group branches;
      int x1,y1;
      Line line1, line2, line3;
      x1 = getNewX(x, y, theta - DELTA_ANGLE, length);
      y1 = getNewY(x, y, theta - DELTA_ANGLE, length);
      line1 = new Line( x, y, x1, y1);
      line1.setStroke(Color.GREEN);
      line1.setStrokeWidth(10);
      recTree( x1, y1, theta-DELTA_ANGLE,
               (int)(length*REDUCTION), g);

      x1 = getNewX(x, y, theta, length);
      y1 = getNewY(x, y, theta, length);
      line2 = new Line( x, y, x1, y1);
      line2.setStroke(Color.GREEN);
      line2.setStrokeWidth(10);
      recTree( x1, y1, theta, (int)(length*REDUCTION), g);
```

```java
        x1 = getNewX(x, y, theta + DELTA_ANGLE, length);
        y1 = getNewY(x, y, theta + DELTA_ANGLE, length);
        line3 = new Line( x, y, x1, y1);
        line3.setStroke(Color.GREEN);
        line3.setStrokeWidth(10);
        recTree( x1, y1, theta + DELTA_ANGLE,
                  (int)(length*REDUCTION), g);

        branches = new Group(line1, line2, line3);
        g.getChildren().add(branches);
    }
    else
    {
        Circle circle = new Circle(x, y, 7);
        circle.setFill(Color.LIGHTGREEN);
        g.getChildren().add( circle );
    }
  }

  public void start(Stage stage)
  {
    Group group = new Group();
    Line line = new Line(SIZE/2, SIZE*2/3 + 5, SIZE/2,
                          2*SIZE/3);
    line.setStrokeWidth(20);
    line.setStroke(Color.GREEN);
    group.getChildren().add(line);
    recTree(SIZE/2, SIZE*2/3, START_ANGLE, SIZE/6,  group);
    Scene scene = new Scene(group, SIZE, SIZE,
                              Color.LIGHTYELLOW);
    stage.setTitle("Broccoli");
    stage.setScene(scene);
    stage.show();
    }

    public static void main(String[] args)
    {
        launch(args);
    }
}
```

Bibliography

[Aho83] Aho, A.V., Hopcroft, J.E., Ullman, J.D. *Data Structures and Algorithms*. Addison-Wesley, 1983.

[Car04] Carrano, F. M., Prichard, J. J. *Data Abstraction and Problem Solving with Java:* Walls and Mirrors. Updated ed. Person-Addison Wesley, 2004.

[Col92] Collins, W. J. *Data Structures: An Object Oriented Approach*. Addison-Wesley, 1992.

[Dal08] Dale, N., Weems, C. *Programming and Problem Solving with Java*. 2nd ed. Jones and Bartlett, 2008.

[Hor14] Horstman, C. *Big Java*, 5th ed. John Wiley & Sons, Inc. 2014.

[Goo06] Goodrich, M.T., Tamassia, R. *Data Structures and Algorithms in Java*. 4th ed. John Wiley & Sons, Inc. 2006.

[Knu97] Knuth, D. E. *The Art of Computer Programming*. Vol 1: Fundamental Algorithms, 3rd ed. Addison-Wesley, 1997.

[Knu98] Knuth, D. E. *The Art of Computer Programming*. Vol 2: Sorting and Searching, 2nd ed. Addison-Wesley, 1998.

[Kof94] Koffman, M. *Software Design Data Structures in Turbo Pascal*. Addison Wesley, 1994.

[Kru87] Kruse, *Data Structures and Program Design*. Prentice Hall, Inc. 2nd ed. 1987.

[Lee92] Leestma, Nyhoff, *Data Structures and Program Design*. 2nd ed. Macmillan Publishing Company, 1992.

[Lee93] Leestma, Nyhoff, *Pascal Programming and Problem Solving*. 4th ed. Macmillan Publishing Company, 1993.

[Lew04] Lewis, J., Chase, J. *Java Software Structures: Designing and Using Data Structures*. Pearson Education, Addison-Wesley, 2004.

[Lew17] Lewis, J., Loftus, W. *Java Software Solutions Foundations of Program Design*. 9th ed. Pearson, 2017.

[Nap95] Naps, Nan, *Introduction to Computer Science Programming, Problem Solving and Data Structures*. 3rd ed. West Publishing Company. 1995.

[Pev05] Pevac, I. *Recursive Examples in Java*. XanEdu-OriginalWorks. 2005.

[Pev16] Pevac, I. *Practicing Recursion in Java*. CreateSpace. 2016.

[Sed03] Sedgewick, R. *Algorithms in Java*. Parts 1-4. 3rd ed. Addison Wesley, 2003.

[Sed04] Sedgewick, R. *Algorithms in Java*. Part 5. 3rd ed. Addison Wesley, 2004.

[Ste90] Stevens, R. T. *Fractal Programming in Turbo Pascal*. M&T Books. 1990.

[Wu01] Wu, C. T. *A Comprehensive Introduction to Object-Oriented Programming with Java*. 1st ed. Mc Graw Hill 2001.

Made in the USA
Middletown, DE
28 June 2020